WANDA COLEMAN

AFRICAN SLEEPING SICKNESS

STORIES & POEMS

by Wanda Coleman

Mad Dog Black Lady (1979)
Imagoes (1983)
Heavy Daughter Blues (1987)
A War of Eyes and Other Stories (1988)
The Dicksboro Hotel (1989)
African Sleeping Sickness (1990)

WANDA COLEMAN

AFRICAN SLEEPING SICKNESS

STORIES & POEMS

BLACK SPARROW PRESS
SANTA ROSA • 1990

ACKNOWLEDGEMENTS

The author would like to thank the editors of the publications where some of these pieces first appeared. *Alcatraz 2, The Alley Kat Readings, American Voice, Angels Gate Poetry Book, Anthology of Magazine Verse, Arete, Bachy, Black American Literature Forum, The Black Scholar, Caliban, California Quarterly, California Quarterly of Poetry and Art, Callaloo, Chester H. Jones Foundation* anthology, *Comic Spirit, Contact II, Dicksboro Hotel and Other Travels* (Ambrosia Press), *Dirty Bum, Electrum, Element, Eleven, Enclitic, Epoch, Essence, Event, Gasolin 23, Gold Dust, Gorilla Extract, The Greenfield Review, Hawai'i Review, High Plains Literature Review, High Risk, Insurgence, Invocations L.A./Urban Multicultural Poetry, The Kindred Spirit/Chiron Review, Look Quick, The Los Angeles Times Magazine, Massachusetts Review, The Maverick Poets, Mendocino Commentary, Michigan Quarterly Review, Momentum, The New Infinity Review, Neworld, Obsidian II, Paragraph 4, Poetry/LA, Prophetic Voices, Rhododendron, Snow Summits in the Sun, Spinning Off, Tendril, Turpentin on the Rocks, UCSD New Writing Archive Newsletter, Venice the Magazine, The Village Voice, Yellow Silk.*

Mad Dog Black Lady (1990) is a revision of the book published in 1979.

This project is funded in part by the California Arts Council, a state agency. Any findings, opinions, or conclusions contained therein are not necessarily those of the California Arts Council.

Black Sparrow Press books are printed on acid-free paper.

LIBRARY OF CONGRESS CATALOGING-IN-PUBLICATION DATA

Coleman, Wanda.
  African sleeping sickness : stories & poems / Wanda Coleman.
      p.   cm.
   ISBN 0-87685-813-2 (cloth) :   — ISBN 0-87685-814-0 (signed cloth) :
      —ISBN 0-87685-812-4 (pbk.) :
   I. Title.
PS3553.O47447A69   1990
811'.54—dc20

90-1294
CIP

For George Jr., Marvin James & Sharon Elaine

TABLE OF CONTENTS

Mad Dog Black Lady 1990

1

2

African Sleeping Sickness

1

2

African Sleeping Sickness:
Stories & Poems

MAD DOG BLACK LADY 1990

1

when it's time to go
it gets dark outside
and then it gets dark inside

UNTITLED

the hit man has oily fingers
formulae for getting money back to its owner
dues collected, a job well done
in the alley somewheres back a little while ago
they found my body and wondered
who what where when and why
how was obvious

    the telling of this secret
    a louis the 14th avenue cement chair
    beneath low ceilinged back room
    fish eyes/me swimming in them/smoke-water
    trying to do things the "right" way and not
    knowing what that is

    this the beginning journey
    life unfolds under the number 13
    you can roll it 7-6 the hard way or 8-5
    i'm fading mars. you can tell mercury where to get off
    freaks don't turn me on

    i've walked down this boulevard so often i've
        memorized the cracks

the whore has cancer of the cervix
question: is it deductible as a business loss?
the payment for flesh is in flesh
in the market it's a known fact that it takes cheap
to get cheap

    it's mapped out beautifully
    those eyes read it all. a mirror of
    artistic temperament calls for withdrawal
    distrust everyone you're attracted to
    flee like the devil from the ones who say
    they love you

this beginning journey
this beauty unfolds under sun of long hours
if i score a hit, it will be the hard way
when the smoke settles — victory
dead or alive

i've crawled into this hole so often it feels like home

the man at the top of the building
threatens to drop to his death. it is my mouth
creaming *jump jump jump* along with the mob, maddened
turn away from the spectacle of crushed bone and gut and
    blood
his artistry spread along the asphalt running into drainage

if it's all the same to you, i'll keep stepping

WHERE I LIVE

at the lip of a big black vagina
birthing nappy-headed pickaninnies every hour on the hour
and soul radio blasting into mindwindow
bullets and blood
see that helicopter up there? like
god's eye looking down on his children
barsandbarsandbarsandbarsandbars
where i live
is the gap filled mouth of polly, the old black woman
up the street whose daughter's from new orleans and who
abandons her every holiday leaving her to wander
up and down the avenue and not even a holiday meal. she
collects the neighborhood trash and begs kindness in
doorways/always in the same browns, purples
and blues of her loneliness—a dress
that never fades or wears thin
where i live
is the juke on the corner—hamburgerfishchilli smells
drawing hungry niggahs off the street and pimpmobiles
cluttering the asphalt parking lot. pool tables in the
back where much gambling and shit take place and
many niggahs fall to the knife of the violent surgeon.
one night me and cowboy were almost killed by a stray
bullet from some renegade low riders and me and
kathy used to go down and drop quarters
and listen to al green, and the dudes would hate
my 'sditty ways and call me a dyke
'cause i wouldn't sell pussy
where i live
is the night club working one to six in the morning.
cigarette burn holes in my stockings and wig full of
cigarette smoke. flesh bruised from niggahs pinching my
meat and feeling my thighs, ears full of spit
from whispers and obscene suggestions and mind full of
sleep's spiders building a hazy nest—eyes full of
rainbows looking forward to the day i leave this hell
where i live

avoiding the landlord on the first and fifteenth when he
comes around to collect the rent. i'm four months behind
and wish i had a niggah to take care of me for a change
instead of taking me through changes. this building which
keeps chewing hunks out of the sides of people's cars and
the insane old bitch next door beating on the wall, scaring
the kids and telling me to shut up. every other day she calls
the cops out here and i hope they don't run a make on me
and find all them warrants
where i live
the little gangsters diddy-bop through and pick up
young bitches and flirt with old ones, looking to
snatch somebody's purse or find their way into somebody's
snatch 'cause mama don't want them at home and papa
is a figment and them farms them farms them farms
they call schools. and mudflapped bushy-headed entities
swoop the avenues seeking death
it's the only thrill left
where i live
at the lip of a big black vagina
birthing nappy-headed pickaninnies every hour on the hour
the county is her pimp and she can turn a trick
swifter than any bitch ever graced this earth
she's the baddest piece of ass on the west coast
named black los angeles

SON OF A

he came in looking for a mama
stumbling off "truenoids"
spreading blue pills across the tile counter shouting
      "bitches   bitches   bitches
        i'm a beautician and make sistuhs beautiful"
silken superfly waves across his cute pate
kiss of sideburns and mustache
zip-down doe leather jacket
black high heel boots and sunset boulevard eyes
shouting
      "bitches   bitches   bitches"
latinos behind the counter suddenly couldn't speak english
little bit started to tease him, sayin'
      "niggah, please place your order"
he was too busy cuffing a customer
      "man i got some truenoid here for sale"
falling down on the concrete floor between shouts
      "i'm a beautician and i make black bitches beautiful"
the door ran into him and busted up his lip
he reeled out into the parking lot
a vicious trouble making wall lumped up his head
he came back in
his fly unzipped, damp with unsuccessful piss
clutching 2 appointment books and a pair of worn
black leather gloves
long tall 40-ish
two sistuhs came in about 3 a.m.
dug him
      "look honey, i gots nine babies at home
      so's i knows jes' what to do for *him*"
told him how he was a man
to respect hisself
put his dick back where it belonged
we watched him smile to hisself as they paid for the burger
the three of them went out to the parking lot's cold morn
in my head i could still hear his shouts
      "i makes bitches . . . bitches . . . bitches . . ."

THE SILVER SATIN NIGGAH RIDES

for Al and Pete who
i never see no mo

together they cruised thru Beverly Hills
"killin' " white folk
laughin' (sippin' Silver Satin and V.O.)
they be partners stoned and angry
cadillac low and wide snatching moonlight

stylin'

teeth against brown velvet skin doin'
a step'n fetchit routine, drinkin', droppin' reds
some purple haze too

Hatred steps out of his hiding place (our souls)
comes 'live

       "Goddamnit man, that bastard's a pimp!"

everytime we try to make love
he lays between us

Hatred he drives movin' thru downtown
breaking windows indiscriminately
screaming bitterly, "yah goddamned muthafuckas"
meaning absentee landlords and
solicitous shopkeepers

then they fade, blending into night
carrying stolen loot home
drunk chatting eagerly
to the fence/a man of leisure and
fat pockets

"Shit, man I swear the bastard's
a pimp."

they move on are moved on
and moving is swift and sweet
another neighborhood another time
molestin' the naive and the slick
with equal zest
rollin' barflies in dank alleys
hopin' to break the spell

boredom and pending dead ends

like chumps they get caught
jail time

meantime that ol' silva satin niggah rides
long lean finely clean takin'
good care of the cadillac until
the boys "raise"
as he licks his chops greasin' down the streets
lookin' for more chumps

they say Hatred drives a hard bargain
but he sold us out cheap

AT THE STOP

virgo stella slips out to give
pussy to cute yellow don
she gets more tips than anybody in the place

security's in tonight/a black cop
named bullet flirts with me in cold of 4:30 a.m.
is honest about his children

fresh out of jail he snatched the chicken
ran into night, "i'll pay you back — i'm hungry"
an old man loaned me $2.20 to keep shapiro from
taking it out of my pay

jesus the mexican cook gets a hard-on
every time i do deep knee bends to keep my legs
in shape and free of varicose veins

the music man arrives on fri's and saturdays
sells bootlegged tapes and $2 wigs to anyone who will buy
his van reads: jive

10½-12 hours slave labor
being urged to eat — help myself
on payday the schlep deducts $6.25

i got 4 hours sleep but no rest
past week a blur
had an accident today — too tired to see straight
home and found insurance cancelled
wondering how i'll ever escape
quicksand
harder i struggle to get out
deeper i go

DOING BATTLE WITH THE WOLF

1.
i drip blood
on my way to and from work
i drip blood
down the aisles while shopping at the supermarket
i drip blood
standing in line at the bank
filling my tank at the gas station
visiting my man in prison
buying money orders at the post office
driving the kids to school
walking to bed at night
i drip blood

an occasional transfusion arrives in the mail
or i find plasma in the streets
an occasional vampire flashes my way
but they don't take much
my enemy is the wolf
who eats even the mind

the wolf will come for me sooner or later
i know this
the wolf makes no sexual distinctions
i am the right color
he has a fetish for black meat and
frequently hunts with his mate along side him

he follows my trail of blood

i drip blood for hours
go to the bathroom and apply bandages
i've bled enough
it's my monthly bleeding of poison
getting it out of my system
watching it as it flows from the
open sore of my body into the toilet stool

making a red ring
so pretty
flushing it away—red swirls
a precious painful price i pay

my man cannot protect me
the wolf has devoured most of my friends
i watched them die horribly
saw the
raw hunks of meat skin bone
swallowed
watched as full, the wolf crept away
to sleep

2.
the wolf has a beautiful coat
it is white and shimmers in moonlight/a coat of diamonds
his jaws are power
teeth sharp as guns glisten against his red tongue
down around his feet the fur is dirty with the caked blood
        of my friends

i smile
i never thought it would come to this

scratching
scratching at my door
scratching to get in

howls howls howls
my children are afraid
i send them to hide in the bedroom

scratch scratch scratch
the door strains
howl howl howl
cries of my children "mama! mama! who is it?"

i am ready
—armed with my spear inherited from my father as he
from his mother (who was psychic) as she from her father
(who was a runaway slave) as he from his mother (who
married the tribal witch doctor)—me—african warrior
imprisoned inside my female form
determined
i open the door
a snarl
he lunges
the spear
against his head
he falls back
to prepare for second siege
i wait
the door will not close
i do not see the wolf
my children scream
i wait
look down
am wounded
drip blood
cannot move
or apply bandages
must wait
wolf howls and the roar of police sirens

RAPPING WITH OPPORTUNITY

i sit at the desk
it feels good sitting at a desk again
good knowing money will be coming in again
opportunity lights up a cigar and smiles
his pink round face is chapped from overexposure to
wind and sun
white faces chap and peel like that
i wonder how he feels about my brown face
it doesn't matter
as long as opportunity sees fit i'll sit
pick up the phone and make a few calls
try the selectric
my fingers glow
opportunity smiles
he doesn't suspect. if i ever get
my hands on him
he'll never get away
i'll kill him and hide his body
under my desk

A BLACK WOMAN'S HOLE

for Audrey Christian

she crawls in it for the only
refuge allowed her. and her children
grow fierce off the acid and piss and cum and crawl out
and shit on the world and die young because the world kills
those who defy it, decry it, seek to change and rearrange it
— all but the lucky the cunning the dumb

there are those who go down into the hole with her
find she's transformed it into paradise

if the world knew it would put her hole up for sale and
        turn her out

DECOR

selling my soul is not the question
there's no market

home: an assessment of torn newsprint shelf paper
ancient enameled stove in need of scrub down
ants feeding on last night's dead beetle
greasy dust thick on top refrigerator
dirty curtains

wishes gather then scatter/eager buyers at fire sale
pain in need—every other word, want

photo: books and manuscripts neatly nestled
under dust in faded orange stolen milk crates
old sun-bleached blue-green divans
a stained orange desk with two broken drawers
cheap masonite wood-look dresser and warped mirror
one fake redwood table with wayward leg
burnt sienna & yellow throw rugs conceal soiled gold carpet
bold canvasses, posters, certificates of sainthood
king size bed in bad need of change

my running sore of effort festers
does not heal

WANDA IN WORRYLAND

i get scared sometimes
and have to go look in to the closet to see if his clothes
are still there

i have been known to imagine a situation
and then get involved in it, upset, angry and
cry hot tears

i have gone after people
with guns

once i tried to hang myself and got terribly ashamed
afterwards because i was really faking it

i have gone after people
with rocks

i have cursed out old white lady cart pushers in
supermarkets who block the aisles in slow motion

i have gone after people
with my fists

i have walked out on pavlovian trainers who mistook me
for a dog

i go to sleep and have dreams about falling
and can't stand the suspense so i sweat it out
and land on my feet

i have gone after people
with poems

i get scared sometimes
and have to go look into the mirror to see if i'm
still here

WOMEN OF MY COLOR

i follow the curve of his penis
and go down

there is a peculiar light in which women
of my color are regarded by men

being on the bottom where pressures
are greatest is least desirable
would be better to be dead i
sometimes think

there is a peculiar light in which women
of my race are regarded by black men

> as saints
> as mothers
> as sisters
> as whores

but mostly as the enemy

it's not our fault   we are victims
who have chosen to struggle and stay alive

there is a peculiar light in which women
of my race are regarded by white men

> as exotic
> as enemy

but mostly as whores

it's enough to make me cry
but i don't

following the curve of his penis
i go down

will i ever see
the sun?

34

TODAY I AM A HOMICIDE IN THE NORTH
OF THE CITY

on this bus to oblivion i bleed in the seat
numb silent rider
bent to poverty/my blackness covers me like the
american flag over the coffin of some hero killed in action
unlike him i have remained unrecognized, unrewarded
eyes cloaked in the shroud of hopelessness
search advancing avenues for a noisy haven
billboards press against my face
reminders of what i can't afford to buy
laughing fantasies speed past in molded steel luxury
i get off at a dark corner
and in my too tight slacks
move into the slow graceful mood of shadow

i know my killer is out there

NO WOMAN'S LAND

they trample on my sensitivity
goose-step thru streets of my affection
line me up before the firing squad of insecurity, shoot me
    down

when the smoke clears
my corpse interred
they sing my praises in a hymn

love politics — a legislature of pricks

they pass bogus bills of understanding
table my lusts in committee
refuse to acknowledge my plea for justice

before supreme court of need

when the fires die
they toss my ashes to the wind
moan prayers

administrative coup — détente for them, defeat for me

they demilitarize the zone of my thighs
napalm my dreams of black womanhood
overkill my illusions in a pushbutton mechanized
    fuck-session

when the dust settles
my hopes float face-up in the
river tears

martial law — immediate withdrawal?

no white flag of truce
no surrender

DOG SUICIDE

on the harbor freeway
heavy traffic 6 p.m. home to the pad
the kids in back and me watching, careful
the front and back
sweating behind r&b at the steering wheel
the dog
saw it standing there
about a mile up
cars/sudden slowing to keep
from hitting the dog
that threatened to
go out on the freeway
i slowed up with the flow
as i passed, it moved
toward me
i honked my horn
it went back, then
i watched to see what would happen
in the rear view mirror
it just walked out there
in front of the black buick
its body fell into a tumble
under impact
its flesh tore red and open
then another car hit it
and another and another
thought about it on
the way home
wondered if that dog knew something i didn't

SOMEWHERE

there's an alley with my name on it
cold gritty pavement
crushed glass
shadows
an occasional thin stray cat
hunting through overturned garbage cans
old tin cans/beer cans/ketchup bottles
cigarette cellophanes
bits of torn paper dancing on an eddy
foot falls stumbling past
lovers in the apartment across the way fucking
argument in the mack den
kids shooting pennies behind crates
in back of the liquor store
a few roaches trucking from the fumigated house to the one
across the street
drip drip of water from the drain
wind rises scattering stuff

i will meet you there

LUZ

i remember you the way one remembers a bad meal. this
evening you belched up from the memory of a thirteen-
year-old black girl whose friends were either misfits
like herself or belonged to another race

i liked you very much luz

enough to maintain our limited friendship though i knew
you liked me less. i was fat, ugly, outcast. the glint
in your eye that hunger that drew me to you
was my hunger also

you spoke spanish

used to teach me some and introduce me to your culture,
food, ways. i knew nothing of illegal aliens but understood
your poverty went deeper than mine. yes, the dimes. i let
you steal them from me

you put me down

that was okay, for there was that to which you aspired/the
whiteness of the white world/a door closed and
bolted to me. you entered. i remained outside

this night i see your eyes

as clear as if you were here now, your full girlish figure
(i had none) was my envy and has probably
gone to fat with many babies or
to dust after many trials. oh luz, i had so many things
to say — so many tight chic referrals to the
latin-black conflicts over white socio-eco crumbs

i wanted to say them through you

all i do is remember, think of us/our people as we were
or could have been — apart, the awful silence
together, the awesome storm

■

he asked if i was seventh day adventist
they were the only kind of black adults
he knew of
who read and wrote
in public

BLIND BETTY

and i used to pal around a lot. we'd go and do and run. it was fun in a way. i mean, i liked betty. she was a-okay. i called her blind betty cause she always pretended she couldn't see me when i knew that she could. i was fascinated wondering why someone who couldn't stand to look at me always hung out with me, always called me on the phone to talk to me for hours at a time (one time eight hours straight. a listening record for me).

perhaps it was 'cause i looked so much like her after the very first glance she felt i no longer bore examination — it isn't necessary to continually stare at one's mirror image. one begins to think strange thoughts.

blind betty and i were both black, almost the same skin tone except that hers ran to yellow and mine ran to red. blind betty wasn't as tall as i, physically, but her ego made up for every inch and she was active aggressive while i was passive aggressive, so it seemed to work out. in that way, blind betty and i were fast friends.

it was cool until one day something bad happened to me. i got sick and i did not feel like suffering through blind betty's interminable monologs anymore. when i was forced to travel miles to work so i could pay my doctor bills i tried to tell blind betty. but she pretended she did not hear/see my mouth shape the syllables. i shaped them very carefully. i even wrote them down in a book and gave them to her to read. but blind betty couldn't see the pages, being blind.

so one day, when me and blind betty went to breakfast with her gentleman friend, i took off my blouse and bra. blind betty saw me. she let me know in no uncertain terms that she saw me. she didn't like what she saw. her gentleman friend proffered no opinion. i drove blind betty and her man home.

i've been free and seen ever since.

41

THE RED QUEEN

i have stepped into the mirror of my hatred and am
cut and bleeding

the blood falls on newsprint/your eyes
come laughing back at me like sirens clearing the speedway
approaching emergency

i do not know what to do about you

that has happened to me with other women and men/
        betrayal
but i devoted eight years of my life
to shaping and sculpting a fine relationship
and now it lays across my typewriter jagged and broken

i was going to spend a hundred dollars of the hard/and
money does come hard for me/earned cash
i make droning away my life to pay some guy
to throw a blueberry pie in your face, but he wasn't into
        vendettas

i have to pass your house every other day and
i get cold chills every time a mutual friend mentions your
        name
memories i had plunged full fathom five bob up and moan
        booooooooo

i cornered your old man, leaning angrily out of my car
and screamed obscenities and incoherencies at him
one day while on the way to work

i told you you were full of bullshit, bourgeois nigger bitch

i fumed and farted and cursed and stomped and pranced and
pounded a few table tops that bruised my palms

in dreams, i chopped off your head, strangled you, slapped
        you and spat on you

i have tried to make my dreams reality by cornering you
on neutral territory, but you know me well
and have avoided me to date

one day our paths nearly crossed and you ran inside and
hid in the closet until you were sure i was gone—i found
out, laughed and tried to dismiss you with contempt

i have attempted to write you out of my system in several
          poems
and in this one i face you head on, but hear only
the sound of glass shattering and not your screams

i whited out your name from the dedication in my first
          poetry book ms

i have done everything but gotten my hands on you, so be
warned. i'm saving up money for bail and i've
been to jail before

BEYOND SISTERS

she loves me i know she loves me she spoke words i
forbade with my sexology and lust for man-flesh
she got drunk—had to get stinkin' drunk falling down
half naked on the blacktop
me standing there my black leather jacket/the boy *he* was
trying to make me believe i was
helpless/pimp-whore games in watts winter night her
fingernails digging into neck of my flesh

> "you mine—you always be mine
> no matter what"

i wanted to do something. a man would've kissed her. i was
        not a man
her passion beat down on me
i tried to tell her i loved her but words got lost amid the
headlights and cold:
windy outside the hamburger joint the dude who had
bought her the half pint got jealous
felt him want to hit me felt his eyes say if only you was a
        man
dropped his arms in frustration
called me a bull dyke moved helplessly away she wanted to
be with me

she cried the words i forbid in my sexology and lust for
        man-flesh
cried cause i wouldn't help her with her baby
which could have been our baby if biology had not been so
        funky
but i have babies of my own
and, granted, a strange woman
woman

night
the phone call silence
she is on the other end calling
if i would say her name . . . if only i could say her name

i hang up

mirror reflects determined set of my jaw. taurus is fucking
with me again. in a while may will be over. perhaps
gemini will be kinder/gemini understands — is like me — both
male/female

she loves me and i know she loves me

       "to the grave," she said
       "you be mine — you be my bitch"

KATHY

cold? no i'm not cold. it's not the wind. it's that damned cat!

there was the time i visited her in the women's facilities.
she had been incarcerated six months.
his ghost. she told me she saw his ghost. he
came to her cell. i knew that things were coming to an
end but couldn't let go. i should've walked away
and said, "fuck it." another niggah bites dust

their love was ugly. forced, stilted, ugly. even their child
was ugly. it was ironic. he died bickering over the
ugliness/their love. a child. abandoned to its half-black
half-amerindian grandmother the whore
in blythe somewheres to grow up hating men just
like her mother. tricking them into dead end streets and
empty wallets. i should've turned away, closed the door
but she was my friend

no. i'm not cold

county jail visits. glass wall between us/her
wig for appearances, in thigh-high ill-fitting slammer dress.
left messages and took messages and left money and tried
to give encouragement. surely a year was easy time to do.
            she
could concentrate on art work. i'd visit the foster home
and she should stop thinking about god punishing her.
she killed him over the baby

at her trial the cops testified she showed no remorse. i
remembered that later when i saw her face to my face
the day she killed me or saved me depending on how one
            looks at it.
that ugly baby crying while me she and he tore up that
raggedy-ass house, fighting. i told her, for the first time,
how bloody fucking ugly in the face she was

please, don't close the window

we will meet again is carved into my flesh, a scar i carry
beneath this mantle, testimony to an event history will
never betray except for that ugly child still living to
reproduce herself across the head of some unsuspecting john
in some sleazy motel room this side of the
twenty-first century. her legacy, a cheap shot shake-a-booty
bumping and grinding in hollywood's pits

when you see me shudder and shiver it's not the chill of
late night air it's probably the memory
twisting around in my brain or some radio
tune in my ear conjuring up the corpse of her and her man
—the one she wasted with a saturday night special—of her
dancing to the boop-boop-ada-boop of soul while he and
me sat around taking drags off a joint
unmindful of tomorrow

no. i'm not cold
it's that damned cat is what it is, crossing my grave

KATHY (2)

1.

rattle those chains restless spirit of
neon and nooky night serpent dreams
black alleys/arteries/ovaries/hands
every pothole crack cranny mouth
she comes into view/memory—nigger whore
hot hot pink halter top 'n short shorts
strawberry blonde wig to match

back i go back—the clock leers. memory's sweet licorice kiss
young blood fast on tomorrow, unsophisticated
brash, belligerent, assuming
fleshy brown thighs in hip hugging skirts
knew how man-tasty we looked
ran streets, waitressed, shared rent 'n' hard times
any luck that fell our way

up against it

bein' runnin' buddies made it better

2.

he tongues her clit/tongues away our friendship

her eyes pursue me
spill over into mine

back drawn back—bitter, i sweat to keep us tight
use every trick i know. too few. he comes between us/her
thighs a notarized contract/marriage/strip sessions and
a murdered man's social security checks

the ghost of hollywood past carries me
to santa monica boulevard and western's
sleazy piss hole shake-a-booty ghetto

it was my car. i drove.
parked outside meat market cooling my ass (i did a lot of
ass-cooling in those days) while he and she went in
he to jack off/watching in wings/"protectin' mah interest"

   on stage they come live beyond stark footlight
   shimmy pastied tits/yellow eyes, chocolate skin
   she barely moves her head, tosses it slow, seductive
   "it makes me sick to see 'em hard and naked" protruding
   from open flys/rods raised in rigid salute
   she snakes and grinds to the drum beat g-stringed hips
   "it makes me sick to see 'em cum,"
   throwing kisses wet as mud

his fingers are still damp when they get back
she's silent, embarrassed, "feels dirty"
i throw gear into reverse and then forward
hit the freeway, wondering who'd survive the crash
if i took us off an embankment

3.
arriving high on reds, angel dust, malt liquor, disgust
pain killers — the moon, an unwilling witness
a few eyes peek casually from behind drawn curtains
she stumbles from his arms, grabs me, stands behind me

      "don't let him take me. can't you see what
        he's doing to us? you're so stupid stupid stupid"

i tell her it's okay — words smothered as his pimp-hands
reach out firmly to subdue

4.
     men are dogs men are dogs men are dogs

her voice intrudes/trespasses on my dream
the clock has changed faces/its hand-arrow
lances my core. her face-mask dances before me/teases

my pulse roars
i reach to rip her open
bust down the dam
free the flood
drown us all
wet shaken anger
sober icy sweat
i wake
cling to damp sheets

kathy i bleed

some loves die hard

THE WOMEN IN MY LIFE

my sisters do not write, unrequited letters beg
        communication
a show of hands (would asking love be too much?)
yellow in new mexico
gather dust in norway
silverfish in seattle washington

they cut

my comrades are men
hard with the wisdom of street, prison, university
sex attraction harnessed by circumstance

she has ass length thick carrot hair/dark brown thin braids/
thick bushy brown kinks teased into an up-sweep
peppered with tiny dry white flowers/blond short
nordic silks/black glossy medusa coils/
she's bald and her eyes eat me

they know better

my sisters do not visit. unrequited footfalls
a path crisp and new with anxious welcome
a silent door

the women in my life cut deeper than the men

2

when it's time to go
money gets scarce
he pays his way and you pay yours

THE MAN BEHIND THE WOMAN

his tongue pursues me through a wake-sleep
hotel neon sign flashes saturday night sighs
parked at service station gas pump
he wants to fill up on my passion — nineteen and catechistic

    he beds me in the book of experience
    turns to a blank page, pens my eyes
    etches in apprehension and timidity

penetrating balm of his musk
incontinent sheets pressed with body-sweat
dark beige curtains adust with malodor
anonymous toilets clamor diverse perversity
                (geo. washington shat here)

    so much older, he does not teach
    i learn by observation: he masturbates
    prisoner of flesh, he regards me through wire screen
    of impotence — i cannot touch him; i have no hands

    yellow lamps — posters — postures — a hug
    thin lips — sociological study in race relations
    ancient lore stored in mindpockets
    gray-eyed jealousy stuffed into secondhand overcoat

    down dark-thighed avenues running handcuffed
    echo cries of platform shoes — my escape. stolen
    cash stashed into bra strapped thinly around heart
    my eyes police matrons clucking over my property

therapy is shooting into empathetic ears
black woman to black woman she's my mother of mothers
understands and soothes; forgives transgressions. i cannot
pray/my gods forgotten — there lies another jungle

    he beds me in the book of experience
    a diary of brief romances
    salient shockley on psycho-genetic binge

his tongue presses me into submission, awakens passions for
patriarchical classics — rings motel buzzer and passes $6.50
      across
counter of my breasts. frees bitch-elephant from its cage

lumbering along hollywood avenue, i seek the savior

MIDNIGHT CARRIES ME SOUTH ALONG
ILLUSION AVENUE

used to know a man who sold it hot. a woman who knew
the ins and outs of bad paper. an artist who kiln
fried ghetto pots and glazed eyes —
a neighborhood of chances

the story starts in brown webbing of palm raised eyes
in supplication. god slur drops reds, drinks schlitz malt
liquor, bumps booty to the blues and swoops the
asphalt after curfew, brim cocked
wide open for action

a chronicle of hearts bleeding, minds writhing, fists
pounding head. call it heads or tails (1866 or 1976)
slavery drives it home into that black woman's snatch.
sucks her teats — milk of generations

my story no different. brother love came up to see me, a
sack of goodies and an empathetic ear. "most sistuhs
who been through what you been through been dead long
       time ago"
uncaps the bottle, pours a song. we toast that
bitch, mother america

alone behind the wheel, his ghost rides with me, sips wine.
"you one hell of a beautiful bitch." memory a hand on my
thigh. another of ladies who lose their demons on the
freeway

chorus:
it's true. ain't no new. a different spice, the same
old stew. a different man, the same old screw.
crack a smile, laugh a while. it ain't the
act — it's the style

midnight carries me south down blue ave finding meaning
at the bottom of an empty cup. reading eyes, leery

not to give up too much. a dime
for the cause and thick lips pressed
to the window

HIS OLD FLAME, LADY VENICE

so they kicked him off the beach
those white boys told him to get his ass out
or he'd never see the light of day again
and he left her behind . . .
we revisited the beach
and right then i knew his heart was there
on the court playing paddle tennis
in the bar he used to own playing chess and listening
to jazz
along the beach walking
into lives of people he used to know
the norse cook who taught him everything culinary
and the spry old man who did nothing
but play tennis all the time
thru his past, walking
the many women he had had, a different one every night
and never found the one to make him happy
not even the ones who paid him to fuck
so we revisited venice
i tried to tell him that i had been there before
listening not an art he's cultivated
so silent walking
the little old petition-carrier came up with her gray hair
tied back in protest
we couldn't help her, being black non-voters
there was the bike man and business slow as usual
though lots of people were biking leisurely
and his friend in the van who recognized me from
         somewhere
thought i was from louisiana
a geechie
they kicked him off the beach
and he kept telling everybody he'd be back
and i knew that meant there was no space for me in
his life, that woman, venice
she had it all

WATCHING

the television on
tv tray by the bedstead, plate of food
fish odor rising and blue cheese dressing
the curling upward of smoke
outside raining
kids in bedroom playing, squeals of laughter
die down as bed time approaches and grabs them
the television, on
black and white people moving in fantastic world
tv tray by the bedstead, plate of food empty
stale smell of cigarette smoke
me in bed, watching—waiting
clock ticks raucous
boom boom boom bass sound of neighbor's stereo below
faint voice of woman yelling in apartment next door
looking at the window, stars break thru the rain
letting up
bang bang bang, cops and robbers on television
the book, open, lays face down beside me
sleep runs away every time i reach for it
i am hungry—feeding time at the vagina
half-naked i hide between sheets
he lays there with me 32 years dead
his corpse shows no sign of life
he can't fool me
one eye is watching television

THEY CAME KNOCKING ON MY DOOR AT 7 A.M.

they had a warrant out for my arrest
"what's your name? where's your identification"
i was half naked so they didn't come inside,
figuring they'd caught me mid-fuck
they were right
coitus interruptus LAPD is a drag
i showed 'em alias #3
they said "oh, well where is she?"
i said, "man, she was staying here, but she
hooked up with some niggah and split"
"ok. ok."
they left
i went back into the bedroom
you were naked and still hungry, curious
"what was that all about"
"nothing"
i laughed, took off the rag i was wearing
eased into the sheets next to you
we started fucking again
but things had changed

ON THE ASPHALT

cars on avenue
swim in wine-wind
hungry flesh hunters
prowl neon lit service stations

    zzt zzt zzt
    static electricity loneliness

four whores in sedan
hit norm's where prospects are good
me a ragged spectre
an angry dashiki and earrings

    zzt zzt zzt
    static electrical sextrip

the t-bone steak and french fries
stare at me over the coffee cup
he's thick-skinned
his eyes make kissing sounds

    zzt zzt zzt
    static electric hum of motel buzzer

when he wakes he'll find
his wallet missing and also the pretty
brown girl who could fuck so good
and wish he'd never been born

HIS EYES INTO THE ROOM

shattering silence a gun full of bullets

this one for you, this one for your lover, this one for me
click click in the chamber — jealousy high

humbuggering ain't out of fashion. evolution will never
make this animal extinct. it's in the soil, air, radiates
down from the sun

his hand pretty heavy metal against my temple
like that i'm into next week pushing up old friends and
newspaper headlines
a seance to call back dead poems

we can run it through the camera until the
celluloid snaps
just let me hear those three little words: *make mine money*

a blend of cognac and cocaine
asking about his difference would make a difference
biting tongue as he shoots his ambivalence into my womb
thrills in vacant lots and bloody tin cans

the son-of-a-bitch is kicking down my door, entering the
room, taking me by the arm, slapping my face, calling
me bitch, shoving me into the sheets

i've played this scene too many times
i must like it

A LYRIC

white-eyes wave across aisle
my name in underground code of poets, muttered

our suffering makes us comrades
flag of truce and a telephone number

ex-suicides, we gather, discuss new technology
not much to get fat off here

they say massachusetts, santa barbara, boulder creek
nix frisco — a silicone fag hag drag

a revolution in green candles and nam yoho renge kyo
rhythm taken captive

(she screams into my ear go back to school — fool
a barren womb indulges self-centeredness)

down the street the black and white flashes caution
this new breed of cannibal digests bone

the angels are revolting in heaven:
a drama done in clap, limp pricks and midnight calls to
          mama

THE LIBRARY

walking his halls—a wonder
explore shelves behind eyes—dusty tales of s. holmes
winter afternoons curled up inside his mouth
a history scrawled in knotted brows

country winters his skin
his hands, leaves falling southern autumn
the endless canyon's cool blues of his smile

1950 lives. 1850 remembered. 1450 dreamed.

(the maidens in his fairytale are black instead of the
        knights)

poems gather, age, grow dry and brittle
crack beneath worn bitten nails

alone between the pages of his friends
reads love never found

the street kid from Watts cries
along the university's sterile hall

the stench of crushed spirit
overpowers

her black guru's disappointment
society's made him a woman. it's making
her a man

"shush it up!"

tired. forced to go
round/under
any entry guaranteed—even the window, burglar
the door? it's barred/blocked
piled high with the dead
and still struggling

                        any moment
uncalled, tears come
flow when not dwelling on money
the lack of it. or communication. the lack of it
or empathy. the killing of it

she's gone back to Dayton, Ohio
i've returned the fifty tapes/her
unfulfilled biography

i sigh, relieved, having thrown off
the stone/my belief i could

write her a happy ending

the tears won't stop. 8 hours billing
tattered lives/victims. insurance? for what
they'll be dead soon. that won't halt

my key punch or the cash flow. won't cause a lash
to flutter. not a bird to fall from sky

any day soon

forced to watch
if i don't they'll slit my eyelids
i won't be able to close out the sun
or blot out starlight when it becomes too intense
or sustain my guise of solemnity
while on the verge of murder

la brea
attempted wade thru the pits
extract myself? it sucks and pulls
my flesh. splatters, splotches
i'm burnt

fears crawl out
from between sheets — my thighs
a dream aborted
the stain seeps thru to the mattress
becomes indelible

       i wake sudden as the door bangs open
       two dapper brimmed intruders enter
       my mind/fever races
       should i scream? remain silent?
       am i strong enuff to take 'em both?
       play it passive?

       which move?

from the tap it flows
bitter into the mug, a head on it
he lifts it to his lips, blows lightly
in anticipation
remembers the salt

behind the bar i wash shot glasses
barely there in my daze and
crotch-length skirt

it's me in his eyes. me smelling of

> *i've got to get out of here at any cost*

he savors it. decides
he'll try a taste

i open my mouth
and lay him waste

> any day now any day
> i'm gonna snap
> the streets/skies are gonna roar
> and rain blood

THE NATURAL HABITAT OF THINGS THAT BITE

cold places
beneath sheets

on the other side of the liquor section
reading labels

sitting placidly on the bench at the tennis court
racket in hand

in the parking lot, falling asleep
while trying to read a book

off the freeway on-ramp
thumbing west

near the warm flesh of a back
sleeping

at the service station
coming to make change

at the music store
laying three hundred dollars on the counter

apartments cluttered with books, paintings
and piano legs

in her stomach as he walks away

WAITING FOR PAUL

in the bar
they play songs about outer space
where people love each other truly
where whores are goddesses
pinball machines pay jackpots
of ten grand and
presidents suck dicks for quarters . . .
in the bar
songs about outer space
where drugs are legal
but no one has the need . . . sex
is looking at clouds moving
love in the eyes of strangers
fame, a shooting star, never fades
outer space in the bar
meaningful whispers
mellow ballad sipped from
a purple glass
the problems of humanity
solved on the unprinted side of a
paper napkin
red light and juke flashing
come in captain zero

YOU JUDGE A MAN BY THE SILENCE HE KEEPS

1.
he calls to tell me something. the something
gets caught and can't make it out
he struggles with it over the wire
my eyes straining to sniff the slightest touch

2.
biting snarling snapping words come out dum-dum bullets
into my chest and blood jumps out on me
and a little gets on him
he goes into the bathroom for a towel
hands it to me, mutely

3.
dialing the phone number
click — he's there on the receiving end
i hear him waiting for my voice
hang up hastily, flushing
he knows it's me

4.
my eyes are trapped in his fists
his mouth shapes the syllables that translate bitch
the scream hides between cold sheets
it snuggles against my thigh

5.
his smile enters the room cautiously
finds its way to my face
stays until i wash

LANDING PLACE

purple red and gold sands endless stretching
his arms and mouth going down
green stars and wine flavored flowers
slipping into the sleeve of madness love
wailing pulse of machine to flesh touching
giving of other experiences and ancient marks
from past burnings

> she left him and that house
> empty
> he is the hall of her haunting
> i feel her there, even when he
> enters me
> i'm not even a sub
> just something until next reality
> a bridge

desert wind blows ears passion gentle
dry lust and hint of sweet possibilities
marriage of loneliness to loneliness
rebounds cacti gray against sun
sipping rhythm and blues bubble bath
crying fresh hungry grinding brown and tan
mind empty cavern and eagle overhead flying
there is a corpse down there to be eaten

> she left him and those car payments
> took the children
> fled deathworld of his love
> another man?
> i don't know/he hasn't told me
> but the odor of her flesh still clings
> to his memory
> she had big tits
> that's why he married her

landscape morning
six a.m. rising to return to factory of life
he lies but i sense he hasn't slept at all
just laid there all night listening to my snore
and wishin'
it was she rising to prepare his breakfast
wake the children/clean house

        she left him in the cold morning
        he came in/everything gone she
        could carry
        ransacked the valuables of course
        this after the fight and she
        had tried to kill him
        hole in the heart of things

call me won't you?
sure i say, moving quickly to the desert
dew glistens on the surface of rock path
mellow sex satisfaction full bodied aroma
you will call me later? he asks
i wonder how long this will last
it don't matter
it won't last for very long
i'm not like her at all

ON THE TRAIN

he's the last train in the station
i've been riding for hours
destination: a publishing party
hope the bones will have plenty of meat left on them
by the time i arrive

people are meals to be digested
stories to scrawl on basement walls
poems to regurgitate

my stomach growls
this might be my last meal
one can never trust tomorrow
she's a fickle bitch and will
betray a niggah in a minute

he's the last train in the station
shuffles and scrapes his way across the
landscape of my sky
smoke stack of passion: a strange conductor
            (blond and gray-eyed)

people are salami, cheese and dill pickles
a whole deli of wild aromas and 52 flavors of flesh
i confess my cannibalism—it's a gift

my mind growls
this might be my last poem
i've never been able to trust my fingers
they always betray my mouth
they complain and steal the tears
out of my eyes

he's the last train in the station
i'm taking him to the end of the line
to a banquet for renegade poets

there will be plenty of raw meat to eat
the wine of fresh blood
and for dessert, souls

THE EMOTIONAL CON MEETS A VIRGINAL IDEAL

don't ask me where i've been
places dark and bloody
you wouldn't want to journey there
and i'm too tired

bearded man in long green trench coat stands outside liquor
store, stops me in excitement of eyes to score a hit with this
tall stallion, saddle and ride her into sensual fulfilling
a nightmare—the cream and she snorts vague interest

>"someday, you'll look back at all
>of this and laugh"

don't ask me what i've seen
my eyes, brown and muddy
you wouldn't want the dying of my
spirit on your hands

bearded black man in red slack suit toting bomb of our
       love's
revolution in black briefcase. an appointment in samarra, i
       say
he stares at the sun, urges devoted blindness—hand to my
cheek in fond caress—the cream, she snorts contempt

>"you're the most beautiful woman
>i've ever had"

don't ask me what i've done
robbery and murder just the start
it's such an effort to make it without
being wired

bearded black man laced in gray kaftan of emotionless flesh
eyes finger meat of his conquest, the stallion, broken,
       stands yoked

in lust for her master, shivers and whinnies against cold
       desert
wind blowing—he saddles up, pulls the rein

        "you can seduce my body, but you
          cannot seduce my mind"

don't ask for explanations
the words are dark, bloody
you wouldn't want to pay the price
of my confession

THE DEUCE OF CUPS

the black would-be poet told me a story
about his cup in the middle of a forest of cups
and how there was a golden cup
it was *the* cup
and how he had found it
and had known that it was not brass
as were the others
and i knew he spoke of another woman
the woman who was half-black and half-ceylonese
who wove spices and spells into tapestries of love
she was his gold flesh beauty with hip-length silken brown
hair. he told me about her as he talked, reached for my
thigh, kneaded my soft darkness and told me i was a
bronze cup in his forest of cups
and cupped my breasts and
his hands worked the bronze, fired it
found it strong yet yielding
he told me gold was much better
but he had lost her
had abused/misused and she had been taken by another
man and so he was content to have bronze
to fill the cup with cum

WET THURSDAY

don't make that kind of book no more
don't go for that cheap kind of ass
short is on, stretch a buck till it cries
it's not quantity — it's class

blues got me. blues done got me and gone. blues in my
coffee. blues in my song

a trickle of blood, a story. early fifties
when *ho*-ing was good. a black man could cut
him a slice of the glory. and let a bitch
sit if in the mood

blues got me. blues done got me and gone. blues in the
morning. blues all night long

his eyes wear the past like a sable
when struttin' one's stuff was the rage
the life of every pimp a fable
pain pussy poverty filling each page

blues kiss me. blues kiss me soft. kiss me deep blues
heart of slavery. blues i weep

she's old. she's tired of struggling
flatbackin' ain't the way to the heights
somewhere other lovers are waiting
other dreams brighter lights

blues got me. blues got me and gone. blues be my trusty
lover midnight till dawn

baby, take a dream if you able
they don't make that kind of book no more
leave the key on the table. don't make too much
noise when you close the door

MEXICO ENTERED THE DOOR
WITH HIM ON THE WIND

came up the stairs and talked to me for a few minutes
kissed me, and took me on the couch

mexico
that place
that whisper with a burp of tabasco
that illusion of tourist bureaus and gunrunners
that twitch behind his smile

he was fleeing to mexico to escape me, the thought of me

mexico played with my big toe and told me to shut up
he wanted to fuck

mexico is a very bad black actor with a hook nose and
strong white teeth/an ancient child whose grandmother
spoke cree and let him run naked in the sun

mexico thinks i want to get my hooks into him
little does he know, my heart is set on jamaica and points
            east
i've been to mexico before

SESSIONS

doctor asked me if i had any sexual fantasies. i told him i
     had none
my fantasies could not be spoken. they would not be well
     received
and he might try to kill me

          reality: him cruising by in his cadillac
          me at the bus stop on my way home to hubby
              and the kid
          he smiles and doubles back, ready as spring
          i slide in next to the singer. at the motel
          he plays hollywood to my watts

the doctor asked me who i loved most, my father or my
     mother. and i
said i loved them both the same, but differently. father
     understood
one side of my personality and mother, the other

          reality: him slipping the ring off my pinky
          unnoticed, then pretending to help me look for it
          he smiles and tells me he's ready
          i slide in under him, unaware that this is
          just another movie scene

doctor asked me what i thought about the face that curved
     along
the paper. was it male or female. i saw a woman there and
     said so.
he told me it could be either. i didn't understand the
     significance
of that particular test

          reality: me showing up on his job
          the blistering anger/anguish of summer. i want
          him to take me and the child away from my
              man

i want him to stake a claim. not ready at all
he avoids my eyes, cries about his wife and
her suicidal tendencies

the doctor asks me what i am. i say, a *non sequitur*. he is
    suddenly
afraid as i spew out my hatred. across the rug stamping
    angrily at
my absence from the nation's tomes. he shifts his glasses
    uncomfortably
hands me a tissue for my tears, tells me he does not want
    me as a
patient. walks out. it's cold on the leather

> *reality*: me running into him a couple of
> years later, after his nervous breakdown and my
> divorce. lust like yesterday cops a feel of
> my ass, and it's to the motel for one of the good
> old days. he's trying to make it back to the top
> and it's my turn to do a fade

the apartment a fist closing round me. i go back to the
    streets, call on
a few friends and assure them i'm okay and no longer
    courting death. didn't
really need a doctor after all, now that i've finally found a
    decent job

TIME COMES WHEN YOU KNOW

suddenly tomorrow is not in your vocabulary. yesterday,
    the constant,
faithful companion. you knew him all along

and now that all your friends have gone, he welcomes —
    does not scold,
and though cold, his embrace comforts. this love of what
    we've done. no
failures, not a single one, but ahhhh — *the disappointments*

       coming home to the mouth crying to be fed.
       it pulsed and sucked: blood, rising from
       his back. a tiny pool of it. the purple
       blotch, a temporary signature . . . her pen
       of pain scrawling its demands across his palm

       how many times did his plea of ignorance
       go unheeded? until finally something
       broke inside

STAYING AND NOT STAYING

thanks to Sylvia Rosen

"Usually, when the man can no longer
support his family, he leaves it"

sex is good but not enough
love, good but not enough good to hold

      they fire him whenever they
      see me
      they do not know he is black
      it surprises me
      many people think
      race prejudice
      ended with the civil war

      he's without a job
      poverty gnaws at us/has us snapping
      at each other/the children

i've been here before. same dream, same moment
the note on the coffee table or was it a key? or both? or a
phone call?

      this time she does not cry. at first
      this time she does not tell her parents
      this time the announcement to the kids is
          matter-of-fact
      this time she will write it down and examine it like a
          scientist
      identify and catalog the sociological and economic
          factors
      this time she will smile until the lines
      become permanent

      he is restless, the restlessness
      of a race
      hurry manhood hurry

    hurry money fame and glory
    we don't have much time
    we born old die young

my eyes catch him feeling bad about himself. his hands
        deny it
his mouth moves to distract me—a kiss or an idle story
i've heard a dozen times before

i break out in hives when i think of life without you. i have
        willed
myself to die within hours of you. i won't make you stay if
        you want to go
my heart is cracking under the weight

        she hasn't changed the sheets since he left
        she's heard of women like that
        places left set, clothes laid out, books turned
        over open as if the reader had just gotten up
        shaving things poised on the bathroom sink
        she even experienced an old creole woman
        who always ordered two drinks and over them
        talked to he-who-never-stayed but never went away

some of us are lucky enough or young enough to start over

husband—something society deems necessary
wife—a high pitched bark

UNTITLED

she was the perfect woman
until he discovered she had a mania for flesh
he'd come in late at night. she'd be gnawing away at it
under the covers

she kept jars of it in the medicine cabinet
and when she kept telling him she had a headache
he would lay there looking up at the ceiling, knowing what
she was really doing

sometimes she'd snatch a bite in public
one day they were visiting mutual friends
she dropped her purse, it fell open. all that red
bloody black flesh on the carpet. it was embarrassing
so that night he decided to tell her that it was no good
over, finished

and as he mounted the dark stairwell leading to her living
quarters he hesitated. but no, he thought. she loves me

she had crouched behind the door, and as he walked past
she sprang

she stored some of the fresh meat in the drawer by her
typewriter. she put some chunks of it in
the bowl by the bed stand so she could
munch on it while she watched tv
she wrapped the rest of it carefully in tin foil
and stuck it in the freezer

looking into the mirror she let out something like a bark
well, she thought, i never lie to them. i always tell them
what i am. they never believe me

3

Art in the Court of the Blue Fag

SWEET MAMA WANDA TELLS FORTUNES
FOR A PRICE

dark stairs
me walking up them
the room
is cold
i am here to fuck
then go back
to the streets

he sighs
touches
likes my lips
my cocoa thighs
we lay down
the bed yields
he comes off calling mama

outside
i count my cash
it's been a good night
the street is cold
i head east
i am hungry
i smile

i know what tomorrow
is all about

BERSERK ON HOLLYWOOD BOULEVARD

these days fat pigeons coo
flap wings, bread crumb anger,
    constipated. plenty of long hairs
    cabaret flowing green candle wax jazz

a spastic jerking borders on rhythm
metronomadic my chest to his i strike a chord
    we are dancers. we dance thru life, thru love
    for a fee, we dance on your grave

the death notice came tuesday
wednesday i had my affairs in order. lazarus in red
    the acid eater deals in children
    proffers his wife to lady cannibals

thick-tongued cotton-mouthed choking
spittle of cancerous mothers dying in polyester sheets
    may her womb dry up. may her nose grow warts
    may her lover yellow and wither like onion skin

as i dialed for help
the phone ate my last coin

ART IN THE COURT OF THE BLUE FAG

> playpoets gather round
> the table. tonight they are carving up
> a macho moist morsel gray-eyed
> sandy-haired straggler in
> celluloid fairyland

in the corner he nods, tries to forget the smell of her thighs
wishing she wouldn't speak. niggah bitch ghost

> smoke red eye nod down we turn on
> to each other each love making takes
> longer more intense rivers run down
> my inner walls he grasps and eyes
> close in rhythm his fine beige frame
> forget the pain gold comfort stained
> in our aborted procreative efforts we
> die together and are reborn at 4 a.m.

the hyena rang the doorbell the stinking meat of our dead
affair squeezed into his attache case staining the pages of
his ms: "i've come to meet your husband. i'm going to
frankfurt with a russian whore"

i'm reminded of another who had to see me before he and
his wife left for spain and another who had to have me
one more time before winging to frisco, his
round of dog food and wine commercials up

they either get too much of me or not enough

dear daughter,

   there is a cut of man who haunts the alleys and avenues
scarfing adventure/pro bums satisfied to spill cum into any orifice
as long as it's tight; who play the game of fame by shattering
the dreams of the children they father. they read glory in chan-
cres, vomit, spit, mucus, tears and blood. they will shove it to

you anyway they can and a month after they've split leaving
you dangling between suicide and insanity, come back to bor-
row five bucks and sympathy. beware. learn the smell of this
man. it's the laughing face whose eyes never smile

        gas heater glow his eyes he lights
        the pipe we fall into step we are
        now leaving hamlin we are now beyond
        the moon stroking bold and cold no rose
        has ever smelled as good as that
        mammie jammie sipping coffee and
        turning on to juju whip it whip it
        i'm water he takes a drink

        playpoets touch blooded fingers
        to yawning mouths. another
        tasty life appropriately spiced with
        liquor, drugs and a pinch of sex
        an adequate and filling meal

at the corner i stop before the flashing red lights. the blue
fag looks out over sunset boulevard and sighs

he is ruler of the realm

ART IN THE COURT OF THE BLUE FAG (2)

twinight earth my flesh quakes
song of long hours laying blues on the counter

reminder, a friend girl who tried suicide. i saved her life
she repaid me by going with my main man

> reds. a pin. three holes. hot water
> down. thigh. moon vomiting blood

i notch each failure with a burn. the eyes of tucson — radio's
lisp or hollywood's houndstooth jacket in nether world of
juke and jive, a blossom — a chocolate poppy smoked
black onto a needle's tip

he's traveled all around the world in the mouth of a whore,
clasps my hand, sighs haiti, praises papa doc. rich, he
owns several souls other than

> blues. ink. three hos. cold water
> up. sigh. into sun snorting snot

she set the house afire and passed out cold on the mattress
high school disco desire sixteen and not a single dream

on the boulevard i watch the blind tap out courage
behind my shades i too am numbed by neon and am
hustling ass for that pimp, success
the blue fag looks out over sunset. smiles
traffic for miles

black eye laced in pancake, she sips seven-up
pregnant with the eighth or ninth
oh mother, you mothers
and just the other week i thought i was
gonna have to crown her with a bottle (schlitz abortion)
           "see my man do whatever he want but
              his bitches gives me mah respect"
numbers. phone numbers. booking numbers. wrong
numbers. low the sixth floor is where they take
the terminated. tonight it's una
           "sis when you say i'm your man, that
              protects you from these flies — these nigs"
slumberers. over malt liquor a discussion on dreams
the gent says money can buy love and reminds me
that marrying a black woman is marrying
poverty. i have no comeback

black clad, she maintains dignity
clutches her purse. he winks viciously.
oh daddy, you motherfucker
and just the other night i
thought i was gonna choke, hatred exploding
on the tabletop, eyes vomiting blood
           "white people buy sex. niggahs can get
              thigh when they can't get nothin' to eat"
stew bubbles over onto the stove. burned
black-eyed peas. pregnant with murder. when
baby comes i will name him pretty poison
and teach him street
           "who's a punk? he's a punk, dicklickin' son
              of a rhino and you — when am i gonna see
              those legs?"
the number over. the pianist turns
to the wall. somewhere the blue fag yawns
and requests that someone piss quick before he
dies of thirst

SPLITZ

our eyes caught the gun going across the counter and we
didn't miss a sip. two in the morning, wine and tired feet

the pre-teen dark pretty haired son of a mexican ho and
sometime niggah gentleman pimp queried me on
astrological signs — a gemini

>   lady. i need to talk with you. i need to
>   find out something that i don't know. i see
>   kindness in your eyes, an oracle between those
>   healthy thighs. let me lay in and talk

no she's never been to paris and mazatlan's a game
eighteen and avenue can show you neon for days

sure, he's seen my face before. others have worn this map
sacred mouthings, the thousand names of god. squatdo

>   lady. i need to talk with you. i need to
>   find out if you have a telephone. i see
>   sex in your smile, smell the memories of
>   other men. please, take me home

it's cold this california winter's morning. the black cat is
creeping up on pigeons glued to the ground

sunup my teeth sticky with passion's paste and last
night's high. his name hammered into my snatch

>   lady. i need to talk with you. i need to
>   find out if you the one i was with last night
>   you look a lot alike. oh, excuse me but she
>   was as black and as pretty as you and god i
>   need my five hundred back

WOMAN EATER

urgency/to know taste touch smell others
gossip? a long ride west to the ocean of his arms
panic/smoking too much lately
hard risings in the morning

she wants to swallow me/my demons, whole

privacy/dried carnations his love laid gently
to rest in the waste basket. having left the "set"
i am unwilling to give them anything except
get-high time and music

she wants to rub my skin until some of the melanin gets off on her

have you ever had a niggah slap you until
your eyes closed/beat purple green blotches
into your skin/have you ever had a cop handcuff
you from behind

she puts my blood under the microscope, examines it

one afternoon 22 and hot got tired of my niggah's jive and
took my kids in tow, hoofed five miles to the repair shop to
get my cad and arrived babies crying, sweaty angry and the
chumps hadn't even started on it

she wants to rip the song out of my gut and wear it in her hair

urgency! shallow breath/narco-solipsism. his hands tight
around my throat. dying beneath zeon. in the fog the blue
fag pursues me yelling, "fish!" gravel has cut my feet
to ribbons but i move onward, upward from the
esophagus of the city

i am crawling out of her mouth onto the nylon pillow

THE WAY THEY FEEL

soft words. he's blowing in my ear, pressing me back
into grass. lost: one pair of african bead earrings and one
orange resin ring. our clothes stained with oleomargarine. at
$10 a fuck, the inmate who ran the popcorn booth cleaned
      up that day

a journey across town. miz white brite by my side
down to ghetto jazz juke having stopped by sistuh
      i-wish-i-wuz
on the way and there, stoned and longing to meet the
      absentee sax player
(hot hot lips cooling mine) high yellow *boo-dist*
we dance, play pool, stir up the local johnsons

never get in too deep: the words strangle and choke/fear of
being murdered. like what's-his-name. the one they planted
      paraphernalia
on. speaking of feeling lost—when you can't make a move
without permission—they might not kill you. might just
mess up your face. no one should put a period at the end of
your sentence. no one but you

laughter. like he had something on the whole human race
the way his beard caressed a thousand bitter memories/
      opium pipe-dream:

    "she was an addict. looked enough like you to be your
          sister. and sometimes
    she had that look in her eyes. the same one you get
          when you go down on me."

rc loves waco carved into the closet doorjamb of a ghetto
crib. place of many lovers gone. he remains, having
seeped into the plaster. she packed up and split years ago,
taking with her his collection of jazz and pain to
barter for a fix

POET AFTER SURGERY

he keeps falling to pieces
right before my eyes

the pieces of his body in the front seat beside
me

i drive, trying at the same time
to keep them from falling out of the car

his hands spill out of the window and onto
the highway, pulling over to the shoulder i rescue them

and then his head, it falls off his neck tumbling
down onto the rubber mat

and his arms, dropping off his torso
limp beside his frame

and i keep trying to put him back together
and drive at the same time

steering the vehicle west and north
putting him back together one piece at a time

they really did a good job on him
down at the butcher shop

they cut out his gut and his heart and soul
the only thing they left were the words, a kindness

and somewhere there is a piece of him in
her bed, rotting

and somewhere there is a fraction of his
mind tied up in a restraining jacket

it's really a problem keeping him together
we lost his penis in west covina

ART IN THE COURT OF THE BLUE FAG (4)

the whine:
bepalmed avenue. long walk, trying to avoid the burger
shack where puberty makes itself felt between the leaves.
crying over the fictional death of the last man on mars

very long and straight it waved, darted to break her open,
slip between the tight/fear of discovery

if i didn't know he was someone else i'd swear he was someone else

the call:
broadway at high noon. nimbus. bus stop and awaiting a
ride home. it is the summer of breaded fried shrimp and
zen beneath the covers at night
so mom & pop won't see

the blood, a light trickle. she was afraid to tell him, so he
never knew for sure if she was virgin

(at $500 a deflowering, he buys them for his boyfriend,
    watches and masturbates)

and when he turned full profile, the pain subsided/journey resumed

i am safe

DOCTOR SPIDER

for Carroll & Vincent

has an office in beverly hills
where he is one of several arachnids who feed off the blood
of kidney failures
he walks into the office with tennis shorts on, sweaty
and hairy and looks
at me as though i'd just stepped out from under
a rock, sometimes
as if i'm the rock itself, raised to crush him/his ego
on occasion he will
hang two cigarettes from his lip and parade, because it's
cool like paul henreid
or malibu with the tall blonde with tits like "melons
crushing my chest" beside him
in the front seat of his mercedes-benz limo looking very
"new york jew" as another blonde put it
he frequently comes into this cubby hole to ask questions
about his appointments and any
messages. and often i am the only one here. he doesn't
know my name and rather than ask it
he looks at me slightly perplexed and spins away. i will be
leaving this place soon
i hope. it's very depressing, coming here day after day
pounding my ass off
another fly caught in the web

DRONE

i am a clerk
i am a medical billing clerk
i sit here all day and type
the same type of things all day long
insurance claim forms
for people who suffer chronic renal failure
fortunately these people i rarely see
these are hardcore cases
most of them are poor, black or latin
they are cases most other doctors refuse
they are problem cases
some of them have complications like heroin abuse
some of them are very young
most of them have brief charts
which means they died within a year of beginning
        treatment
sometimes a patient gets worried about his or her
coverage and calls the office
i refer them to the dialysis unit caseworker
a few of the patients do bad things. for instance
some of them might refuse treatment as scheduled
sometimes they get drunk and call up
the nurses or attendants and curse them out
sometimes they try to fight the attendants
because they feel neglected/afraid
sometimes they wait until the last minute
to show up and it is the last minute
most of the patients, good patients,
quietly expire
i retire their charts to the inactive file
a few more claims i won't be typing up anymore
they are quickly replaced by others black, latin or poor
i make out crisp new charts
and the process starts all over again
the cash flows and flows and flows
so that the doctors can feed their racehorses
and play tennis and pay the captains of their yachts

and keep up their children's college tuition and
trusts and maintain their luxury cars
for this service i am paid a subsistence salary
i come in here each morning
and bill the government for the people by the people
for these patients
i sit here and type
is what i do and that's very important
day after day/adrift in the river of forms
that flows between my desk and the computer that
prints out the checks
there are few problems here. i am a very good clerk
i sit here all day and type
i am a medical billing clerk
i am a clerk
i clerk

ACCOUNTS PAYABLE

i've been reduced to rubber-tipped fingers
shuffling tons of invoices
a debt that remains unpaid
the auditors have arrived
and the ledger of my sweat, closed
appeals to accounting
go unrecognized among the columns
and day after day the figure i seek to identify avoids tally
at the bank they whisper when they see me enter the line
another withdrawal
my days here are numbered

TO THE ORIGINAL POET

last night i saw another you
at a poetry reading
and got a chill
a lot of tall lean young men with southern drawls
hunched into "hard" life
cursing cunts and flirting with homosexuality
or the needle
a new breed of gutsy alliteration
who spit in your ear about "real" life
and the sons-of-bitches making it
hell — *shit* — heaven — anything but purgatory
and i thought, "there must be a school of them"
like marlin in the waters of this generation
hot in the wake of yours
snapping at fame's bait
hungry for the hook
yet wrestling to be free, once caught
and this one, this spare white brown-haired
son-of-a-texas sea bass seemed to be going slack on the line
he reeled on the stage/page
drunk with beer and expectation
flopped through his poems like some
dying water baby on the sand
the audience was amused and enjoyed him
because he was good and because we'd seen
his act before and it is funny
i shook his hand and departed laughing
i once played the part of cursed black cunt to
one of your carbons with a tennessee walk
who's managed to do quite well on paper
almost as good as you — except
he loves beer too much to commit suicide

ART IN THE COURT OF THE BLUE FAG (5)

the vacationing clerk is on her way to santa barbara
to recline by the swimming pool — one of
california's most luxurious hotels and you
absolutely must dress for dinner

> at cousin mary's i marvel at the years
> etched into her body's arthritic lines
> a pretty young thing she was. and laugh
> to myself, wondering what mama must have
> thought when she ran across those photos — ones
> with the negligee

the stargazer is on her way to new york
there's a restaurant where writers minor and
major gather to jaw over the empire and
she knows she will meet/become someone

> staring at the posters and magazines
> nudes stapled to the walls and ceiling
> my old neighborhood seems even poorer
> than when i left
> being so close to it, even the stucco weeps

platinum laced, the photographer is on her way back to
        roma
the villa where beautiful tanned young men and women
wait to exchange their bodies for a shot at fame
she invites me to visit whenever i "make it"

> night over the campus tennis court. i'm
> alive, so far. wear my crown of holly wood
> feel it tighten around my temple like the lion's
>   jaw/bite
> blood down into my eyes, across my cheeks

on the billboard overlooking sunset, the blue fag reclines
in london he/she's all the rant

THE WOMAN AND HER THANG

she kept it in a black green felt-lined box
liked to bring it out to show people, especially the men
she was sexually involved with
it was a creature she loved
sometimes when she was alone, she'd take it from its box
caress it gently, lay it on the bed, watch
it glide easily over the blanket
frequently she would feed it a mouse or small rabbit and watch
for days, until the lump in its torso dissolved
it was more than a pet
of course, she never saw herself in it
she felt she had so many more dimensions
she was warm and it was cold
people loved her but they were afraid of it
the only thing they shared was a blackness of skin
and a certain rhythmic motion
one day she was showing it to this man
a very special man
a man she wanted to fall in love with who
seemed to be able to love her, a man different from
the other black men she had known
and so she opened the black green felt box
reached in and took it out
gently she carried it over to the bed
where he lay naked and waiting
she showed it to him proudly
he was appalled, shocked, frightened
he jumped. he scared it.
it took a long time for that lump to go away
many times since she has considered getting rid of it
but after having invested so much time in the thang
she couldn't bear to throw it away
a friend suggested she sell it
she's into that process now.

WORD GAME

once upon a time, i a poet, transformed myself into a poem
i was very happy
my line was intriguing and audacious
it could take many forms—a gun, a sword, a heart that
       throbbed
a hand gentle as a kiss
it could express any emotion i sought to convey, as well as
i could master it

then one day i was published

now i do not know whether i am a poet writing a poem
or a poem writing a poet

ON HEAVEN STREET AT ONE A.M.

his mouth liquid this glitter night beneath stars
hollywood squeezed into a dress of blue light and rain
        rutted asphalt
being rousted by car city cowboy's ridin' range
i watch, my eyes about to fall over zero's edge
panic. i'm afraid. four years of fear
taking deeper gasps for air. fighting off the beast

he's thin and crisp as a brand new *c note*
i've scratched that itch before. hairs stand up on the back of
        my neck
tuesday midnight/pulling over to the curb—red eyed/lights
        gone wild
he flashes thirty-two and asks if i have a license to kill

all the stores closed as usual. this sprawling hick town
where prophets of false discovery carp over flesh of the
        fallen
i step cautiously over discarded bones/dreams diminished to
        level of
discharged chewing gum/semen, cig butts and smog
        inspired sputum
this jane of shades, looking to clip the neon phantom
to score big—to rip ass wide open

home waits. and his arms/promise of happy demise and
        well-worn mattress

these eyes in the sky are lights from stars long burnt-out
long gone cold

DEAR LITTLE BOY

in lipstick and nail enamel
ears pierced, mouth pursed in perpetual kiss
promised to a heads or tails cruiser
i hear your mother works the docks in frisco
and your father's home anxious
waiting to count your
night's take

VERMONT MEETS MELROSE

on the corner they go to The Stud
well-muscled flesh riders mount the counter
lean-hungry lusting for hard against hard
and i trek by, about closing, on my way
home from a nightmare revisited to
find eyes probing this alien form. *female intruder*

> "don't the fish-bitch know this is he-man she-man
> territory?"

and i slump under the vibes/eyes
fists beat my back as i suddenly become
aware of my ass, how broad it is and shakes
and is soft and casts a shadow
like the moon

the cross is ready. they have made it strong, electric
neon shocks the night. in the morning they return to work
as if nothing happened

listening. the ladies talk
they *know* life/america
i laugh, the one who knows how well
illusion can kill. the one with the scar that is her body
the one who plots secretly against the
platitudes that keep them sane

      "i bet abortion's gonna be the hot topic this year"

their minds. where did they
leave them? most of my so-called "sisters"
make me ashamed. misinformation
a security blanket of "i-don't-know"
most can't see beyond their cunts
whether straight whether gay

      "he's a doctor & *my god* we can't even afford a
         house!"

didn't they ever tell you christmas was a lie
there is no santa claus. jesus wasn't born on that day
maybe not at all. that there are places where the
children carry knives and will eat a grown-up
in a minute to survive or blow themselves
and their enemy to bits in the name
of freedom?

the ladies talk and talk:

      "goddamn, there goes my nail!"

      "that new bathing suit is darling but i got one just
         like it on sale . . ."

"i'm so tired of taxes — paying for welfare makes me
sick"

on the avenue
the sergeant calls his militant
young nappy-headed soldiers to attention
olive drab against black skin. "we'll be ready
when the *next* riot goes down." a weekly ritual as
boy and girl march side by side. a drill team. with brooms.
sieg heil, baby, sieg heil!

on the seventh floor the blue fag looks out over wealth city
bends beneath his crown of thorns
suppresses a yawn

4

*the world was just an overstuffed toy box
and the piper blew tenor sax*

THREE TREES

lemon:

        we could never
        climb you
        standing like an
        impossible challenge
        with prickly limbs to tear
        black flesh

peach:

        whenever mama wanted a switch
        to beat us with
        she went to you
        shaggy you who belongs to us
        black folk now
        who used to belong to the white
        man named Castro and his boy
        who drew pictures of cannibals on
        the garage wall
        before we integrated the
        neighborhood

fig:

        we used to climb you
        and play peter pan
        i would be wendy and the
        little white boy up the street
        was peter
        the neighborhood changed and more blacks came
        we used to climb you
        and throw rocks at the
        ratty little bastards and some of your
        fruit also

BLACK DUST

to be dust
to be dust
i want to be dust
sepia earth the wind blows
down faded ghetto streets
past walkers
     cryers
     screamers
     dreamers
i want to be dust
whirling along with the fumes from
cadillac exhaust
settling in liquor store windows
getting black children funky
riding on the breeze
thru rat infested yards
down alleyways
catching roaches by surprise
burning in the eyes of winos
i want to be dust
escaping my body's prison
free from pain of loneliness
free from eyes that watch,
from hands that finger
ME
i want to be dust
       to be dust
       to be dust
and
just
blow
away

COLLAGE

summers
summers
summers
afternoon's ripe peaches
lemon loneliness, longing for school
beneath green fig tree and silver man-made craft
winging westward
sunday rides with mom and pop in new green oldsmobile
      super 88
north south east west
church sometimes
me in yellow or pink singing solo
piano recitals and cousin's birthday parties
mama talking about beginning of flesh-smell
deodorant pads and sanitary napkins
picnics in sandy parks, beaches
out of town where no white people go
but not allowed to swim 'cause of nappy hair
days laying in bed consuming/hungry adventures/romances
in volumes/lore/novels
my world shakespeare
        bertrand russell
        ray bradbury
        arthur machen
7 a.m. television shorts of hitler and the a-bomb
gabbing on the phone to last semester's classmate
i learned how to swear without flinching inside
barefoot, tight jeans
smacking bubble gum
green soda & cheetos
lifesavers and rock 'n' roll
eyes of men and boys say, "you're a woman"
watching scales climb upward
pony tail & chinese bangs
roller skates
cooking supper 'cause mom's too tired
me & baby brother older but sitters come and go

hundreds of pale white moths on hot summer stucco wall
in the kitchen chasing mice with the broom
morning's red sun through oil cloth blinds
man next door peeking in my bedroom window
drive-in movies with ham sandwiches, barbeque potato
          chips
and hot cocoa
oxford shoes, bobby socks
suppressed itches
vitamin C tablets & cod liver oil
summers
summers
summers

COFFEE

steam rises over my nose
against this night
cold empty room as wide as my throat; eases/flows
river a mocha memory from aunt ora's
kitchen. she made it in the
big tin percolator and poured the brew into thick
white fist-sized mugs and
put lots of sugar and milk in it for me and
the other kids who loved it better than chocolate
and the neighbor woman used to tell her and us
it wasn't good for young colored children
to drink. it made you get blacker
and blacker

TOMBOY

they caution on trees
do not climb them. limbs leave
scars irreparable by time
and daddy is a leg man

the boy up the street brings comic books/an
offering. my altar/eyes mock
the fright in his blind blond
i can out-bike out-skate out-swing
and out-fight anybody on the block

gang. fists hover around me
vacant lots and dodgeball summers
hooting at the pastel skirts & ribbons
as they giggle by on their way to sunday school

papa tells me how unladylike it is to swear
besides ill-mannered and my dreams
are haunted by whistling women and crowing hens
a bad end on some distant future avenue

fear. i haven't met him yet
and supergirl my name scrawled
in loose dirt across the face of the boy
across the street who likes me but i hate him

nobody violates my territory
and lives without a black eye

i'm the biggest baddest game hunter
in the jungle stalking tiger tiger

young butch and spit on the world

YOU HEAR ABOUT THEM

ones who turn face to wall and die. poverty starts in
at the root. gnaws, rats behind the wall/skull
silence radiates from eye/soul/socket so thick you
smell it when you enter the room of their self-imprisonment

        aunt jessie you were so small
        so sunken into the bed. shriveled

dullness/a glaze: nights endless rocking
last year's christmas cards
and stained antimacassars. dogs so ancient
walking a pain. but young ones are worse —
they're full of the new day

        they buried you on top of someone else
        in the all black cemetery. i visit in reverie

peace that frightens. death should culminate in
satisfaction. hungered to death
wanting material things. dead 'cause he couldn't afford
to dress you fine, dine or chauffeur you around
in the shine of steel over wheels

        he remarried a while after. her heart
        broke tending the shell you left

they come and go now and again. hunger withers them up
want turns them ugly before half grown
the old ones pass quietly
the young ones haunt a room for years

STARBOUND

she walks up astrological stairs
her future, she says, is out there
and starbound,
gazes at pin pricks, hoping
her hand extended to me—will i follow?

        aunt snooky had been dead
        three days before they found
        the body
        she had run away from her husband
        had run into the streets
        no telling what had happened
        had gotten a bad horoscope that
        morning . . .

pausing, the star in the phone
glimmers
a scorpion reclines on my sofa
shakes its stinger at me
we look like brother and sister
somehow i don't feel as deadly

        aunt snooky boiled water on
        the stove
        angry, she couldn't have any children
        a barren black woman
        positively unheard of—his ex-wife
        had his children—
        she boiled water and thought about
        her womb

taurus has paid me a visit twice
and each time he asks me to marry him
and both times i said yes and we got married
and the relationship became difficult
for me

122

but taurus says he loves me so i guess i'd better
accept it, his is the only game in town

        don't remember the funeral
        my last memory of her was the
        time me and taurus went over to
        mom's and she was there
        she took his hand and put it on
        her huge tits
        "feel my heart" she said,
        "it's stopped"

walking up the astrological stairs
suns and moons behind pale curtains
eyes and lips of a woman who kissed me once
bejeweled black fingers, nightmare of womanchild
taurus opens one eye curiously
"is there something wrong?"

"feel my heart," i answer, "i think it's stopped"

TEQUILA SUNRISE

ladies of the avenue
speak of blood

the kid in the yellow organdy dress, that's me
a mirror and innocent to the bone
i told on him, "that nasty boy keeps looking up my dress"
his father laughed

it's time for mating he said
spring and he gets that restless feeling
head up for action. maybe go down to that place
one we was at that night i forked over four hundred
and the dark afro across the aisle came alive

turning off along dark roads
wound me up in trouble and a cell block at sybil brand
a black leather jacket stuffed with woe
handcuffed to the door anticipating those mean bitches
what was waiting

her eyes kept popping up
ice cubes from the bottom of my glass
she tried to tell me she wasn't a friend
she tried to tell me a lot of things

and down on the block they say
that's one hell of a stallion
and she don't need to carry no weapon
she can kill them with looks

124

COUSIN MARY

goes way back to the days/my father a young man

central avenue his pride that tore down cobalt blue
plymouth struggle buggy and mom slave
to the sewing machine

pops used to babysit me/take me for rides everywhere
beside him staring out the window at all the black faces
making tracks
that was where the cotton club used to be
and the bucket of blood. do you remember when
nat king cole played on the avenue and
the dunbar hotel where all the high steppers
went
saturday night like after the joe louis fight or on leave
from washing down the latrines of world war two
at the chicken shack greasin' down
with the black stars

that was before "we" had tv and pops was hot stuff
selling insurance. used to take me everywhere
i was *his* little girl (till baby brother got big enough)

we used to climb stairs/big stairs at golden state insurance
and my dad important, suit and tie—would prop me
up on his desk and the office people would
come around and say how pretty i was
all done up in pale pink organdy with taffeta ribbons to
        match
pink thin cotton socks and white patent leather shoes

she goes way back/those days/wide-eyed impressions

pops would take me to visit
her dancing with the gis/boogie-woogie'n to
some dap daddy ticklin' ivories on the spin of a 78
playing cards and talking that talk

me a little bundle of grins
looking up at all those adults/trying to swallow it all
with my eyes. she was so fine
a warm friendly smile making her home mine

years later done in — arthritis and bad men
doing for those who can't help themselves and barely able
to help herself. selfless. a beauty so deep
gift of inexpensive ash trays to be remembered by/gold

her song to me across years

AUNT JESSIE

>   she wanted pretty fine
>   china, lace, silks, mahogany
>   furnishings rich with age/comfort

she took to bed. lay there for years cracked and torn
hypochondria someone said. one day she couldn't get up
        anymore
it wasn't a game/futile protest against her man/black man
        unable to
give her moons—not even a new bed to lie in
illness came in earnest. stayed

>   'tis said quadroons, octoroons and
>   fair good-haired high yellows live
>   grander longer lives than darker kin

on the visit, mama went in with the other ladies/church
        members/friends
outside the parlor i kept my eyes busy—studied the worn
        leaves of bible
plaster of paris lamps, faded pink shades
tiny round tables nesting figurines, ash trays, candy dishes
the silent electric eye of the tube crouched in a corner
her twenty-five-year-old radio gurgling gospel. a breakfront
of assorted never used serving platters. doilies
the brown beaten face of the rug. vacant candelabrums

>   "there are people like that,"
>   mama said, "who can't live without.
>   don't you be like that"

called in to see her i didn't know the tiny woman
could not hide my shock (which, i was told later, pleased
her) the grayed yellow skin, frail pencil-like bones

she smiled and i hugged her, afraid i might break
        something

her touch was fragile, shattered across my shoulders
she smelled of old bottles of tonic/medicines/ointment/toilet
      water/white
roses dying in the vase on the bedstand/sheets damp with
      sweat of her
fever/eyes rheumy red—freckled hands fell away, released
      me
i mumbled the right things for a fifteen-year-old to say
wished her well and hurried out

      she always wanted. things
      turned her face to the wall
      died

GHETTO MOMENT

he's there, sits very still barely breathing waiting for my
reaction to his intrusion into my life . . . waiting to make
me fall in love . . .

dark room with roses—a few petals fallen against the
hardwood table—a few on the rug. heavy drapes and stale
air. i am old, and this ghost persists in haunting . . . a
black lady with memories of many lovers . . .
tomorrow's diary, today

and he is there behind the old chair, his cobwebs fresh and
spidery—touches me from his grave—a notebook full of
clippings and crypt worms

oh auntie, what were they like and why did they leave you?

she pats me on the head. i slip away, my jump rope trails
behind me. in the garden, fresh roses and sunlit rooms—

a passel of young boys

AN OFFERING OF PAWS

> i was choking her
> she begged for mercy
> a problem unresolved

i was waiting for the end of the story
the big zeros of my eyes mirroring belief in a friend

friend. what is that? the dog that trails me home each afternoon
from school. a big brown german shepherd. i give it no name.
no food except the occasional remains of my sack lunch. it never
leaps upon me, but tags along happily and barks when it first
sees me. and i smile, pat it a little. but when i reach home it
cannot go past the porch. it knows. mama won't allow. dog turns
away. some mornings i smuggle breakfast to dog who waits and
then walks along beside me on my way to school. three weeks
pass. one day dog is no longer there. i never staked a claim.
lonely walk home. i miss dog. hope it has found a better friend.
maybe a home

there was a married one who talked with me. the animation of
our eyes gray blue darts striking a black board one by one hard
fast tongues coming out intermittently, quickly. the tongue of
marx/lenin. the tongue of guns and overthrow. the tongue of
want/possession. over the lips. a thirst for self-determining.
youthful spit that burned images into rose palms. i thought we
would talk like that always. but he had a better job than i and
over the years traveled a lot. i married and lost my job. i call
once in a while or drop a line but there is no response. something
about letting sleeping dogs lie

> arf arf you dog you dog bitch
> i'd like to run over you in the streets

we were on our way somewhere when i spotted her beneath the
wig on a chilly afternoon's bus stop wait. sight took me back.
back to that shabby rear house she rented. back to the draw-
ings she did — the ones i tore into pieces. back to his arms/their

130

arms/arms strangling my mind with ideas too mean to speak, my eyes bulging at what i was commanded to do— out of my skull; the pressure pushing pulsing my skull the two of them/her teeth like needles, my tongue thick as baked fish moving against my lips. *niggah why don't you die?* and i wanted to stop the car and get out. my heart was in my fist. all i could do was stare. "what are you staring at?" he asked. "nothing. i thought i saw someone i used to know."

> babies, i wanted to get them a dog
> but pets are against the lease

worse than jackals they sponge and i work for them. shuffling papers that total more than six figures per month/ghouls/they go in and out and ignore me/one of the filing cabinets. this double duty is breaking my ass— headaches, backaches, blood. a mass of tissue expelled. work dog work sprint around the track. feel the curve. scent— pick up that scent. rabbit ahead. rabbit ahead. slave niggah, slave. eyes find my back. the timid sniffing of a poodle. i am big and black as a doberman and if i come up suddenly in the night, not easily seen

> i would curl up on
> the floor and allow
> no one to pass

bones are scarce these days. the trot down zeon lit cement lanes among the hungry gets me little. sometimes the half-eaten body of a cold hamburger or a warm night's lay on a castaway throw rug. pat pat pat. the losses form rhythms as my eyes search the faces for a kind one. getting too old to meander. time to find one with a fire. one who hunts for pleasure instead of game. one to go home with

BEACHES. WHY I DON'T CARE FOR THEM

associations: years of being ashamed/my sometimes
fat, ordinary body. years later shame passed
left a sad aftertaste. mama threatening to beat me if i got
my hair wet. curses as she brushes the sand out, "it's gonna
break it off—it's gonna ruin your scalp."
or the tall blond haired gold/bronze-muscled
lifeguards who played with the little white ones but gawked
      at us like we were lepers
sound. the water serpent's breath: a depth as vast as my hatred
skin. my chocolate coating. the rash gone now
as a kid i couldn't stand the drying effect water had
coming out wet, cracked and sore all over. one time
i caught a starfish, second summer after my divorce
"i'm not into beaches, or riding waves these days." the only
      time
i like the beach is when it's cold hostile and gray. i feel
kin to it then. or at night. when it speaks a somber tongue
only the enlightened perceive. when the ageless mouth joins
mine. when soft arms caress in timeworn gentleness. or the
poor man's beach, where bodies echo my chromatic scheme
from just-can-pass to pitch-tar-black. at home among fleshy
rumps, tummys, thighs,
breasts jiggling a freedom our hearts will never know
sound. eternal splash. a depth as vast as my love
beached. i turn into the blanket. urge him to fuck me. he
thinks it's corny. i get mad. i get up, stomp away, kicking
the sand . . . while he was with her i was on
the beach wishing he was with me . . . at the beach
aware of his hands urgent to touch, take me before we
return to work/our separate lives . . . here. i watch
you swim into the crest. i'd rather sit and sip wine
enjoy the wind than swim or wade. i smile secretly
at thinly clad slappers-on of lotion/a potion to ward off
skin cancer. in my fantasy i would challenge the ocean
a feminist ahab stalking the great white whale. harpoon it
and ride down down to meet davy jones, content
for my america dies with me

sound. swoosh swoosh the scythe. a depth as vast as my vision
i could live by it, pacifica. learn to like it. now that you're
with me i might even let you teach me how to tread water

NEW LEAF

her lungs emptied out fear. they were black. classic unhealthy
blackness death brings — like a butterfly dehydrated before it
could burst the cocoon, like a body burned beyond
recognition, that new leaf sprouting upward, curled
a sorcerer's wand/pagan/phallic

i stare at it

time stops. for the dying, designations have no significance.
monday blue monday could be any song. each minute
resembles the last, biding until that very last minute
at first wishing it would never come/suddenly impatient
longing for this dream to dispel — to wake into whatever
awaits the dreamer. whatever birth — whatever welcome

i stare at the clock

she gave them all she had. her apartment. her money. her
bed. her innermost thoughts. her laughter/smiles. she
even loaned them her car, her clothes. fed them — she
liked to cook. she entrusted her life to them
like a simple child and they took it and dashed its head
against the wall, beat it and stomped it till bruises
opened and there was blood, bluish red agony staining
plaster and wood. they left. the child, very still.
in that room. nothing but the labor of breath. not even a cry
        for mama

i stare at it. go over to the plant. grab the leaf. break it off

ABOUT FLOWERS

1.
running gag about carnations:
he brought them to me in the hospital with the first baby
red and white pink and coral striped
poor, we worried about medical debts
the county picked up the tab
i still have the baby
he and the carnations are long gone

2.
the old costa rican woman downstairs mothers them
i pay rent here too, more than she
but they're her *ninos*. she complained
time the roses were full bloom
i came in stoned and angry at one a.m. and
slapped them around like bad brats
later that morning she cried over the fallen bruised
pink white and yellow petals

3.
miniature gold heads
dead daisies rubber banded together
he stuck them in the lower half of an old crystal
perfume bottle/a gift for me
pretty for a few hours atop the stereo's plastic lid
every plant that comes here dies

THE LAYING DOWN BLUES

sometimes i get the blues and want to lay down
morning comes like fifty men with clubs — all on my heart

sometimes i get the blues and want to lay down
my lover laughs at me and splits my world apart

sometimes i get the blues and want to lay down
never get up out of bed again
that's the time i push sorrow aside, get up before
the mirror, force a grin

       the corporate man don't have no time for love
       he's banking body on the dotted line
       a contract, the merger's tight
       he's got a plane to catch

       never mix business with business

sometimes i get the blues and go south town
night comes on like fifty whores out frying meat

sometimes i get the blues and go south town
for a lil' barbeque and a friend to eat

sometimes i get the blues and want to lay down
all my troubles in the bed of the police

that's the time i think of prison bars/gray
endless dawn with no release

       the artist man don't have no time for love
       he's banking booty on the game of fame
       a contract, the money's tight
       he's got a snatch to plane

       pleasure is as pleasure does

(money cums, quoth the simp)

sometimes i get the blues and want to lay down
take it to the beach and spread it all across the sand

sometimes i get the blues and want to lay down
take it to Congress and spread it all across the land

sometimes i get the blues and want to lay down
let a draught of phenol make my end
that's the time i push sorrow aside
get up before the mirror. force a grin

SIDEWALK

initials, footprints

whenever i arrive you're there waiting
stretched to greet me—hard firm familiar
how many times i've broken my mother's back in childish
game received a wadded welcome
of unwanted bubble gum

i've always liked you
against my ass on cool summer evenings
still full of sun/warm and fun to lie on and listen
to the distant thundering hooves of steel buffalo

barefoot is how i love to receive you on cold icy mornings
you harbor a newspaper, a feast of bread crumbs for
pigeons or crushed and dying roses
glistening dew drops

sometimes the face you wear is that of an old white woman
gray cracked withered, chock full of arrogance and
abuse—stories i will never hear

times when you rear up and buckle in protest
strewn with glass and blood—testimony to crime
stains that persist

i have run down you to escape
listened to the slap of my feet in flight and later
laughed to find pebbles and bits of glass embedded
in callus/i am ready for you

there are dark metropolises where you dominate
reign omnipotent amid masses of crawling steel concrete
brick final and endless as death.
where the poor, old, blacks, yellows and browns
roast in the steam of your summer, freeze in the
unmerciful snow

of your winter—lapse into lives gray as your yawning
     distance

i've been few places where you're yet to be
it seems you go on forever
will be here long after the city shuts down

and then i discover you bent and cracked by hungry roots
pierced by colonies of ants
broken under the pressure of high-heeled shoes
pot-holed by the rush of rain water from gutters overflowed

HIS HAIR

i am ever picking it from my body
a small pleasure
it is as straight as sweden
mine, kinky africa, catch his, ensnare and hold
i find strands trapped as i make a braid/free them
a few tickle my armpits like his tongue
or in the bathroom
i find them tenacious fingers entwined down south
in my pubic hand
and time to time they make their way
into my mouth

TODAY

today is me and friend girl macking
why we haven't made it if we'll ever make it
about the wrongs "they've" done us—one's loved
today is my man and his *main man* cutting down a pound of
     columbian
                  in the living room
it is my son sick a week with the flu
it is my daughter wanting to help me make hamburgers for
     dinner
today is one week's eve of the anniversary of my finding out
i had a miscarriage somewhere along the way
it is spring/los angeles spring and clouds threaten rain
it does not fall
today is parking my ass in an upward mobility
     restaurant-bar
for two hours jawing over the world
while tomorrow sits at home beside my typewriter
waiting to be written

las turistas negras grandes

my feet kiss the pavement on castillo
a vendor tosses tripe and chicken parts over the fire
azteca gold eye winks sweat beads
la joya la joya (this joy in the streets of la raza)
we are natives of tunisia
we are hunters of obsidian
we are incan gods mad for the blood of our oppressors
pain in abalone butterflies
wide-eyed indian girls in hip-length earth brown braids
today there was a minor revolution being conducted

wind against the rocks
sea sucking the shore

INDIAN SUMMER

we suffer heat
lying down
too sapped to move
locked in by sun
and empty pockets
words come
explosions or not at all
we're at each other
can't touch
the skin sticks
baking
this oven of ancient wood and
no ventilation
the fan hums
unkept promise
we'd rather be elsewhere
he finds his way out
i'm stuck here
with the children
the television
too hot to complain
too whipped for anger
wish there was something else
i could take off

AFTER HIS FLIGHT

we're back to square one
begin. try. a new job. a renewed effort
winter is coming (he's restless, i'm uptight)
august, his smile gone, there are tears
wrenching boy-tears becoming a man
anxious to snatch the world; steal it
bring it home stuffed in a vase, note attached:

> this belongs to us
> right now. i give it to you
> love

around us, sky clouds
turns gray angry protest
blots out the sun

the freeway, she smiles
din/hum/lullaby of spinning wheels
late night traffic whispers hurry hurry
palms guard our passage
ancient orbs scope the window shades
as we douse the light

24 HOURS UP

day. brings the heat of success
i'm on to it and into it. he follows
doggedly, a tooth brush and a razor away
from reality. we have weathered storms
and made it into port battered but intact

> baby when i'm high it's you
> clinging to my ear like a
> big yellow tropical flower, you singing
> in my womb/a chorus of trombones

noon. my eyes on the clock
i'm all over it. beating it. my hands
pound away at the keys, briskly, a minute
away from fantasy. the streets below are full of
limos, mannequins and stars plated in platinum

> baby, when you're down on me
> beating into my heart like a
> big bass drum, you, clanging
> in my head/the bells of los angeles

evening. my head in his arms. our light shines
here. salsa mexicali wail from the neighbor's
stereo, screaming low rider's brakes. we had a rough-tough
day, but made midnight on schedule

BREAST EXAMINATION

1.
in the shower naked
he bends to suck
milk life
urge engulfs
we tumble into stream
barely able to separate
closed in by the enamel fist

2.
before the mirror
he comes up as i look at myself
cups them and squeezes
they jump up hard
nipples in dance-ritual
he's to my back
enters
later i have a mirror
full of hand prints

3.
laying down his arm makes a
pillow for the right one
fingers grasp flesh
he leans forward
takes the left one into
his mouth
bites gently
wakes the eagle
i take flight

BOJACK SAM DEALIN' MAN

see evil speak evil do evil

my weakness as medium of exchange
creates this figment for personal gain — an uncouth
overly verbal spasm belching up street wisdom
a flash of diamond pinky ring and a tooth fairy
who moonlights as a goldsmith to one who savors
psycholagnic tales of welfare class ennui

offers up a first kiss free, perhaps a second and third
but after that you pay thru the hole

a double dicking

and there's just no way to fake the experience

he's a metaphor i'm stupid for (mania to be in)
this fantasy fad coolly immune to
temptations i offer (see me use me as i
need using not abusing) as a sentimentalist
believer in the power of good pussy to hold a man

and his hair, longer than mine, tempts my fingers
and his eyes seducing my imagination
tempt me to love

what i can't have

what appears so real at midnight vanishes
in the chilly light of 7 a.m.

leaves behind a pair of shoes size 9

AFRICAN SLEEPING SICKNESS

1

prophets say shadows sing
night is mother of all learning

BLACK MADONNA

screaming legions/her children chase her down shame street.
they stone her lover into flight. they violate all
sanctuaries. there is no place for her to hide. fouled/her
breath is foul, her hole is foul, her soot skin ashen with
filth — pustules and granulating sores. biblically speaking,
she writhes in manifest pain/forsaken. plagued. the
       screaming
legions of her children tear at her breasts and partake of her
flesh. they slit her consciousness that she may never sleep.
she of the night of nights. she conceived without vaginal
birth/without woman. unclean. she — the victim of victims

father, the crucifixion did not take

GEORGE 1914

twinight

boxed in by shadow. in the corner he dukes it out
with shades

travels the avenue nowhere looking for
not finding

where are you opportunity? knock one more time—
give me another shot at it

(that golden-crested bow. that ship forever never coming in
remember the money tree i made you one birthday to prove
metaphorically it does grow there—dangling from brittle
lifeless limbs)

october will love you as no one loves you

george the wind. hear the wind sing your praise your face
          gone
gray with light/buoyancy of the expectant voyage ahead
that glory yacht to the jordan of your dreams

          way down to freedom land

george hear my psalm my hymn
to honor you as i have honored you all the days of this
          breath
bestowed on me in part—the half of my spirit that is
yours/you

          "for us in our 70s it's too late," said the gypsy. i
          wanted to argue. she silenced me with smiles

it is twinight. the moon is full and plum
i howl to bring back the dead

AL 1968

i stole away those summer nights to lay up in his arms
and after deep drags on a joint to jazz masekela
his eyes would glaze over and i thought it was the high
his head moving in quick lyrical jerks to the sound
his gaze off soulwhere as i lay silent watching smoke rings
wondering what he got out of marijuana and where the
music took him back or onward to perhaps that
west Texas mudhole wishing there was something
i could do to liberate him from the pain
i sensed under the smoke where i couldn't reach
but felt we could fuck it away and sometimes we did. now
precisely at this moment i'm with him there twenty years
ago the smoke the smell of hopelessness so pungent so
unforgettable how he'd turn those ominous eyes on me and
admonish

"babe, it's all bullcorn"

THINGS HE TAUGHT ME

how butterflies kiss

        how to walk like a pink panther

music as religion

        shortcuts across loneliness

always light a joint at the small end
inhale deeply
let the smoke fill your heart

HYDROQUEEN

chilly chilly the air bleeds drama
as our hero does talc
our heroine is sober, courageous in her disappointment
it snows

       (he does not look back and
        she does not vanish)

it is significant that each detail be
remembered. that each dream be analyzed for clues
the psychopathologist digs soma and
who knows what discovery may save
womankind?

        he moves off/evades
        diminishes x macroseconds
        she wants to chase him
        her feet and blocks of ice/movement
        suspended

        little cocktail ice cubes/her eyes plunk
        into a glass atop the counter
        of a south city soulspot

the snowman offers money/the chill of compensation
he wants to help her but
does not warm her bed

        "i want you for everything *except* sex"

today she does not feel below her waist
coolly observes her paled discolored sloe in the glitterglass
she feels puffy and frostbitten

the opportunity to bleed is gone/iced over
she is

substantially able
to get on with her doings

she has learned all there is to know about the cycles of
water

STARVED FOR AFFECTION BLUES

let me in your kitchen, lover
you sure got lots of pots and pans
let me in your kitchen, lover
you gots so many pots and pans
there's plenty plenty butter, baby
come on and let me fry your hams

let me in your bedroom baby
let me wash your dirty drawers
let me in your bedroom
let me wash them dirty drawers
so loved starved for your goody
going down against the law

refrain: take me to your heart
       take me to your home
       take me in your thoughts
       don't let me live alone
       when it comes to lovin', you know
       i'm comin' tuff cuz baby baby baby
       i can't get enuff

let me suck your toenails, baby
i love your dirty feet
let me suck your toenails, baby
you sure gots dirty feet
there's plenty plenty toejam
and it tastes so good to eat

QUOTH THE RAVEN

the room, coolly luminous. a frayed pop-culture rag open
to the crossword. the telephone comes into view/mocks
its body blacker than my skin blacker than black

dry heaves between jags at 3 a.m.
shortness-of-breath. it's humid. his impatient footfalls
at my chamber door. his arhythmic knock

we do a Franki & Johnny. he accuses me of
done-him-wrong
i'm nevah to call his home nevah nevah unless
impending blood or death

so what if they're stompin' my butt down at the factory
and i need a good lovin' fuck to maintain (baby baby please
don't leave me please)

he makes me wash my face. he strokes my hair à la *tell
daddy all about it*. i beg defense/some good game
he opens his fly, cock up
won't i open my mouth to rest and relaxation?

i can't be nice. he smells of her
"is sucking your dick so essential?"
he calls me a choosy beggar. "if you can't go down
we can't get down," and zips to go

on my knees again

"i need more than sex. i need you," i boo-hoo
a severe case of rocks-in-my-head blues

viciously, he grabs me by my kinks
"don't be silly"

that door, baby, i still hear it slammin'

OF NO FEATHER

(but you see, when we discuss birds
you must understand. i didn't know she was cuckoo)

on the night it happened he awakened from a
very deep sleep

(and though we hung with the same flock
from time to time we weren't that close. she
made their breaking up sound like the usual
hen-rooster thang)

she had gotten out of bed without his knowing

(she knew she'd have my sympathy. she tried
to straighten it, telling me she loved him down
to the tail bone. he was a nigger artist
after all. her nigger

my erroneous translation: she supported
his sad bad habits)

they'd smoked a joint and made love
you know how that goes

(but you see, when we discuss birds, i was the
pigeon. she told me he wouldn't be faithful
knowing i'd assume the worst and indict him based
on my own negative experience with like type
the muthafuckin' bloodsucker)

years later
the truth winged by
on the song of a sparrow

he couldn't stay with her after that. knowing what
she was. he couldn't take it

(she sure played me for a turkey)

one night he woke from a deep sleep. she'd left
his side. he listened for her absence and in the
closeness of the tiny apartment he heard the flutter
of bodies in the bed across the way and heard
the whine of her six year old

"don't play with my pee-pee, mommy. i don't play with
        yours"

DEATH 213

this time only one body on the divan

rhythm mortis/soul creep/holed out
this time no limbs askew
(she believes in
tidy endings)

one electric eyeball winks dingy melodrama
overhead a blues beacon
sweetly radiant heavenward. this time

the silent stereo. a bass monotone pulses up from the
apartment below
penetrates the floor

> woman causes fizzle in suicide attempt
> turns on the gas then empties
> her mind

this time beyond novelty
this time beyond television. this time

no bruises. no sigh/sign of solipsistic violence
mere limp pricked resignation and terminal relief
(she loves him she always
loves him always)

no blood pools. no semen spills
no rape no murder no needle
this time there's no chance of schematic mishap/discovery
by friends (nobody evah drops by 'ceptin' strays
sniffin' for pussy)

nuthin'

but cold lifeworn flesh and the rugless bare waxed floor
the obscene intrusive electric eyeball

this time
it is painful/slow
laying stares on the ceiling/rampant thoughts
seeking bone-soaking rest and fetal sleep
the simplicity of carbon monoxide
and headlines

       the pathologist will note a last meal of
       bile and Sartre

this time. no tears no rush no sting
no thrill of expectation no finger pops no do-wops
no so-longs no you-done-me-wrongs

and this time. no savior

LOVE BANDIT

i'm in a place where there are no thieves
i think

so i go out into the slaver's night
to join new friends and leave the door
to my cell unlocked

when i return i know instantly someone has entered
and gone. he's left behind evidence

an empty wine glass

it shimmers in the center
of a barren heart

DREAM 28

the ace high avenue queen of shades
does a bodacious silhouette in burgundy & blue

fades

the magnum opus of screeching brakes — a discourse in
hit & run

this sedition of the flesh

her light in the kitchen window is to let him (whoever
he is) know she's in
to stop by for a little mayhem

(i'm at the sink washing grails
listening for that dragon's roar and the clank of
armor mail & mace)

she will go to sleep arms open
and awake to find them full

DOE EYES

unblinking. dazed

her pearl her beauty
meant nothin'

startled. she was cold-cocked. shattered
wind-strewn glass after collision
legs uncrossed

close on twisted mettle

what alcohol has to offer. dope. perversion.
crack-up and grasp (even straws are at a premium)
he got next to her that fucker fucked
over her best (ever and always)

she fell to earth, thru it
and only ash came out the other side — ash and night

just tell them, wherever you are, only the stupid
are innocent

> he busted your cherry
> he turned you twice
> he knocked you up and out

she did not recover from his truth. it destroyed
her

time has frozen and glazed over. see

a wood in the babe. lost there. lust there
and where are you now, "lady"

waitin' at de edge of de void. waitin' fo him to
whispuh in his sleep, "i'm sorry"

waitin' for words which, unlike the end of your world
never come

CHOCOLATE CHIP

She was browsing through the shelves, looking for items of need. She usually sent the kids to the corner liquor store, but there were some things one had to be an adult to purchase, and she didn't feel like taking time to write a note subject to the lazy misinterpretation of some resentfully underpaid clerk. She needed some aspirin. She needed toilet paper. She needed some cookies for dessert. She needed a packet of safety pins. She needed a friend to talk to. She needed a good fuck. Slowly she selected the items available on the shelves, musing over the latter two. She didn't have a man and she didn't have a telephone. As she stopped she became aware of the flagrantly sexual jazz fusion bursting from strategically mounted speakers. *It's makin' my ears wet,* she thought. *I've got to have that.* At the counter she asked the clerk who the artist was. "Oh, that's Roy Ayers — on his latest album." She memorized the name as he rang up her piddling little score on the register. He watched her slyly, studying her breasts. She looked at him. "Say, Baby —," the big brown barrel-chested clerk grinned, "how much do *you* cost?" She took offense, "I ain't no whore!" she said as she snootily grabbed her bag of sundries. He leered and barked after her as she fled from the store. "I know what you are. You think you too good to sell *it.* You prob'bly givin' *it* away to some niggah now. You nuthin' but a chippie. A chippie!"

dancer in the window

perform for the world may it knock at the door come in
and stay in her halter top and second skins she finds her
      sway
between the notes/rhythm and blues funky butt and jazz
she is the chorus girl at cafe society a boogie woogie at the
bucket of blood a debutante at the black Elks hall formal
      ball
a g-stringed pastied licorice lust a bikini girl on the brass
monkey bar a bottomless kitten in glitter cage under strobe
josephine baker in paris hungry eyes fish nets and bananas

she separates the cotton from the boll

THE CO-STAR

she liked his scenes best. he, his sephardic darkness, his bluesy lips she imagined were the color of pomegranates. she was enthralled by his jawline. no man could wear a suit so magically/majestically. if only she could touch him. if only she could let him know how she felt. his eyes were october sunsets. the flare to his nares sent thrills thru her. after months upon months of black-and-white viewing, shamelessly eager even for the reruns, she could no longer contain herself. one night, when alone before the television (no one else saw what she saw, of course) they went for a close-up. she kissed him full on the mouth. at that moment she became brazen. he kissed back.

ARS POETICA

he came down the mountain
with a full growth of beard, smiling
the new MS taut in his mitts
precious gold of months of solitude/thought/work
he'd done it — conquered the bitch muse
made a nympho of her
begging at his boots to be taken
he felt proud. proud as any man who can
wear pain well
he showed it to his old lady, the black chick
who'd had a hard life. a woman with little mercy
in her heart and less in her vocab
he unwrapped his dream carefully, cautioned her
to wash her hands before touching a single page
after a guttural sound from her throat
she obliged, angry at having her
chores in the kitchen interrupted
he sat her down and read each event. when he
finished, cast eyes to reel in her expression
"how do you like it?"
she watched his hope dance. "that what you went away fo?
it real nice for some poetry"
"is that all you can say about it?"
"no. i could say more"
"well say it — for god's sake, say it!"
she took off the sanitary napkin she was wearing
and plopped it on the page
"needs more blood in it"
and went back to the kitchen

his woman his party his price

it was another great party
plenty of literary hangers-on at the ol' timer's
waiting for the clown show to jump off
a little lightweight repartee
jokes old as grandma moses and beer, plenty beer
me in my wig hat, leotards and jeans
high heel sandals, checkin' out some gray boys
checkin' out the action
the ol' timer is swilling beer and spewing curses
he's been watching his lover, the curlicious blonde cowgirl
flirt with a hot aryan range rider
he's done with it. he throws a bottle of beer
against the nearest wall. there are squeals
of delight. the party has started
and now his curses are louder and she boots over
to calm him down with no success and now everybody
spills out of the kitchen, bathroom and bedroom to watch
"hey" a fat young dilettante yelps
spilling beer on his belly, "the ol' man's at it again"
i figure it's time to split, go home to watts
i find my friend bonnie who invited me to this farce
say adios and then slip out the front door
the old man's disappeared. when i get to the
driveway on the slope of the hill, i see him in his volks
the ignition is whining. it won't start
he looks sad. he looks frightened. he's drunk
"hey, ol' man, you can't get out
you're parked in," i yell as i saunter past
on my way to my pinto
the ignition stops. i look back
he's slumped over the wheel
a man in severe pain. a man bawlin'

BEYOND BAROQUE

there's thangs and thangs

we all sittin' around in a circle. we all come to the workshop to get down and do the thang. and so the leader say "go." then they all start to pull out their thangs. one-by-one each thang is discussed

and somehow, because i'm foreign/new to the circle they keep skippin'/passin' over me. at first i think this is an oversight but after two or three passes i know it is deliberate. they are afraid of my thang. they ain't even seen it yet so i know that sooner or later they gonna have to get down to dealin' with my thang. and when they do i intend to make them regret how they've ignored my thang

some of 'em start jerkin' their thangs and some are just diddlin' with they thangs. their thangs are cute and precious but they are little thangs. in fact, wee-wees. soon they are tired of playing among their own thangs. so at last they turn to me and say "show us what you got"

so i reach down and expose my thang. i have a very big thang. i have the biggest thang on a woman they ever did see. they are not only upset and embarrassed but envious because they think anyone with a thang that big got to feel more than a person with a little thang. and because they have treated me so nastily i flaunt my thang outrageously

i brag about its copious cum. then i say how many who've put their lips to my thang say it is sweeter than honey and twice as runny. and since we's all naked and looking at each other's thangs they hard-put to argue. somebody says some bull about the merits of subtlety. well i can't help what the thang looks like. i was born with it. one woman she say the larger the thang the smaller the brain. but by now everybody know the lie

173

done been put to that myth. somebody say something about quality over quantity. but in my thang they come together
.

     i proceed to put a spotlight on it to make sure my thang is unforgettable. i say how my thang can get so stinky it'll clear a room in less than a minute if i don't wash it proper and i cap it off by saying it takes a big thang to do a big thang. they faces turn red. and then i point at all their little thangs and laugh till i crack

MS. PAC MAN

video fever comes late. i am found

in the neighborhood family arcade dropping quarters
i race the phosphorescent yellow critter across the diagram
eating dots as she zooms
something in this computer chase sweats me
it's not a game i'm good at—neck and arms tensed
tongue against teeth
i've gulped the cherry raspberry, orange and pretzel
once i scored the apple, but the pear and banana elude me
i can't stand being watched by better players
when the pastel spooks trap my glowing yellow self
i curse loudly and ignore the stares
i'm careful not to blow many quarters—even this
engrossing little chase is luxury—
my metaphor my life (the harder i play the lower i score)
as the board promises a goal of 5000 points plus free
       game—
too little for too much effort i pursue my dramas/those
tasty shimmery blue spooks bursting into points i'm certain
will put me over
but don't

BRUNO

washing six-month's worth of dirt & the devil off
        the old car
        is cheap stress therapy
the front window on the passenger's side
        was shattered by a vandal
        twice this year
the first time we had the money to get it
        replaced. the second
        time we didn't

we keep it parked across the street in front of
        the movie studio
        sound stage
it's a 1968 Buick Skylark we bought together but
        it belongs to me
it was towed away once. we had to cough up a
        few hundred to
        cover tow fees
delinquent registration and a ticket gone to warrant

what's she doin' drivin' a rogue's car?

it used to have a stylish vinyl top which has
        cracked and
        peeled off
when driving the jagged edges make a strange
        flapping noise like
        retreads about to blow
what's left of the paint job suggests metallic green

        now it's primer gray
        cracked and blistered
        dented in spots

the tires have been borderline flats for some time
        we're careful never
        to drive it unless

absolutely necessary. the transmission has a leak
        it needs fluid
        every 7-10 days
the rear brakes are shot, the radio/tape player defunct
        altho the black leather
        interior is still nice
if dusty and worn at the rear window deck & speakers

i maintain it minimally until the day when we can
        afford to either
        restore or replace it

i wonder how long it'll be before it's stranded
        in an intersection
        and has to be junked

like my raggedy hand-to-mouth

BABY I'VE GOT THE REDS

drams of men night heat i sleep rut hard nipples & cold
fear

she went crimson in class
blood appeared suddenly and unexplained thru her skirt
running down her coffee legs, spotting the waxed wood
        floor
she screamed and screamed
and was carried away after all attempts to calm/to convince
her it was normal, failed

my womb vacuumed scarlet of stubborn life
one more birth/a sentence of 20 years hard labor
aborted
i tough it out legs astraddle, feet stirruped
watch the child-stuff drain into the glass cradle
freed

old dried up dread brick consigned to building
no longer lusted for/no man needs
warmth held by stone but nothing blooms
children point in unnamed terror, flee
her sorrow/rheumy orbs/swamps
as she turns to say hello

baby—i've got the reds

PRESSING THE FLESH

we and me on a go-and-see trip up to the promo
pow-wow the movie producer has done a comic kowtow the place
is done in phony smiles business cards and spineless guile we
wade thru the shades and slicks to do our do see who is who
and maybe baby if the vibes are right there might be a sexual
liaison tonight

i'm strung out on excess success and slightly short
on glib finesse but i try my shot at a connexion keeping business
business for my protection i'm sipping champagne fizz when
mister movie man gets it up to give us his impression of semi-
artistic smart-mouth expression when an album cover floats by
and a pyramid of cocaine catches we's eyes

we leaves me and goes out back while i sit and play
social pitty-pat i think it's really nice to snack and chat and sip
but this kind of crowd gives me a natural fit i locate we say it's
time to split put-out cuz i didn't get my share of the hit put-out
cuz i didn't want to be publically snooped doin' it and that little
booze buzz scored wasn't worth shit

HOLLYWOOD ZEN

anticipation as good as actuality

       tall palms, jacarandas, pine and eucalypti.
cathedral light refracted by stained glass. perfect weather
perfect mountains perfect sky. what's a little temblor
once in awhile. days of undisturbed median summer. the
sumptuous textures of shadow and shade

endless stimulation to arousal

       sleek autos in a riot of colors. speed, thrilling to
it, the power of deserted freeways at night. soothing
blue green waters hot tubs and whirlpools. casually falling
into a good thang, money coming easy. the promise just
at the fingertips, just within reach. panoramas impacting
like sloppy wet kisses

success: bullshit with the proper stranger

       the politics of clear eyes, capped teeth and
manicured smiles. tanned skins bared for show. lean trim
muscular pumpings of iron, sweat ecstasy. navy blue
uniformed keepers of the obscenely sacred. like power, age is
a state of income. someone to discover someone to make
a star of. blueprints for happiness designed by spiritual
architects. *ahhhhh*

orgasm after orgasm after orgasm

       rest relaxation recreation and ritual. image
matters more than substance. something mystical, akin to
bliss, haunting, beautiful. all it takes is desire and a
little elbow grease. what's imagined for tomorrow means more
than what is past. complexities demand three-hour
lunches. creativity is the art of contentment with
compromise. what starts as a cry ends as a song

the rhythm of life is the run of the jogger

NOISE

           slake in decibels. take me up

central city soulsound swing
           siren sing/police/ambulance/fire
canned crescendo of tv laughter
who long be heard
(they who make it least complain most)
neighbor murders neighbor over too loud stereo

           a band rehearsing their way out
           of poverty

           the phone prrrings
           to fill my ear
           the latest scam of
           a hungry friend

concerto in cement major
a cacophonic symphony/no way traffic/helicopter hum
buses buzz. the discordant roar
as jets descend from kingdom come

baby cries/the future seeps into a good night's sleep

           muzak

drag racers backfire and burn rubber
the collision of lowriders at hell's intersection

still morning's crow of a lone engine
kicking jack frost

           oh say do you hear a scream
           victim's hymn
           heart thump thump

the mating moan of a stray cat
the stoned shuffle of junky feet
vomiting at 5 a.m.
the frantic dance of domestic pests

gunshots entering
wounding

longing for the eden of her birth
the neighbor woman from Guatemala
chronically waters the dirt
nothing grows but mud and mosquitoes

SEÑORA MOSQUITO

she winds her way into our darkness
ignores me
in her thirst for his blood
often i wake to his screams and curses
as he chases her into my dreams ·
the next morning he grumps, "i was up all night
with that damned mosquito
i'm bitten head to toe"

about señora mosquito he does nothing
and i grow angrier by the night
then we argue then we fight

it is not that i don't understand
once, as i dozed, i was startled into alertness
by the roar of a turbo jet at the tip of my ear

i bought insecticide
sprayed the trees and bushes outside our windows
and the sills inside
angry he declared the spray more harmful than she

but she stayed away two weeks

i bought repellent for his skin
he refused it

i threw the can at him
he left a bruise on my arm

finally
i bought screens for our bedroom windows
she stayed away a month
only to return
to plague him last night

it is his blood she lusts for
still he does nothing

and now so do i

WHERE THE SUN DON'T SHINE

i may get by to see her on a Saturday. once in awhile i'll run her somewheres. you could say it's dark down there. i try to offer up a little light.

sometimes on my way if i'm in pocket and ain't in too big a hurry i'll swoop by a liquor store and pick up a bottle of concord white and some cigarettes for her. for the life of me i don't understand what ties me to her. bullshit. i do too know. it's how we see life. we see it the same.

it's rare to find someone who sees everything almost exactly as i see it. and that's what i gets from her—what i see. she sees as i see. not eye-to-eye but eye-in-eye. so it doesn't matter that she has so much less than i (not that i have so much—i don't), but that i can walk around on this earth knowing there's at least one other human being who validates my vision.

so i put forth some effort to pass a bit of time in her company. beyond friendship beyond respect—it has to do with history. our assignment on this planet. what has given me shape has given her similar shape. forces that've battered me have likewise battered her. and while all of this occurred many thousands of miles apart separated by a decade we've come to meet each other in this place this darkness.

there's an emotional shelter in which we harbor one another against the ferocity of living. she is ladylike, articulate, dignified. i'm sullen, smart and haughty. being the elder she may occasionally assume a motherly stance. but my being the more insightful in some ways often causes her reliance on me for explication of some circumstance beyond her grasp.

when i'm down she lifts me up and if i can when i can i return the favor.

and we both get the giggles when we gaggle 'bout *niggahs*/men—our favorite subject: ideal niggahs low down dirty niggahs niggahs past and future—husbands sons muthafuckas. men with power men without. what to do about for with to our men. the best a man can do with his what's-it/tongue/lips/style and do. and i likes to get high with her. likes to get tore down

185

and laugh and cry with her. likes to amen and teach and help me fatha have mercy on my soul with her.

i likes to take her out of that hole she lives in for a couple of hours to sit up somewheres and pretend there's possibly something good in our futures (that we think we have a future is positive in itself) and chit-chat and look ladylike and ignore or tease the attention of men-eyes coming our way — whatevah.

and don't let us start gettin' down in the mouth about white folk aka current events. we can unload much shit about them and the trick they've put us in. there's no end to that steam. with her i can blow some of it off. and not just that either. whatevah happens to be stickin' my behind at any given moment. and while we rarely come up with solutions (cuz ain't none really or it's come too late for us) we at least provide one another solace is how i looks at it. that's lots these days. and while she's anxious to get out of the neighborhood i actually enjoy going down to see her. to slide back into my step/rhythm/language. after talkin' proper all day so's to be clearly understood/not misinterpreted i'm hungry to get into mother tongue. and after holdin' myself in the stiff posture survival demands it feels too good to cut loose.

these days 'bout the only time i can is on visits to see her.

funny how anywhere from a half hour to three hours max can sustain me for months if need be. while i frequently complain about givin' up time to what she wants (like chasin' her check on mother's day) beneath it all i kinda like being able to assist her through this life. like myself i know her trials have been many and difficult and that she's lucky to have survived. we both know we're lucky to've lived to this maturity and neither one of us is long for this life so long on grief so short on happiness.

like i said, *solace.*

i have to fight the trash to get to her door. little kids be standin' around lookin' like wide-eyed African hunger posters. so if i got it i go into my coin purse and make like Christmas. her neighborhood is a tough one chock full of gangsters. poor working folk and county welfare folk. she gets by on a little taste from social security — having reached that age.

and like she hasn't been doing well these last few

years and her decline has been marked. unable to work. losin' her teeth. losin' her butter. i pray she ain't gonna quit on me cuz i would sorely miss her if she gave up the ghost. and that's funny too cuz i've had more than one occasion to curse her name but had to ultimately swallow my pride, back down off my high and mighty attitude and forgive her her trespass.

so there we be sittin' up in her crib which these days is usually one room stinkin' of twenty years of roach spray and bad plumbing, walls of crumbling plaster, a rug worn brown from the infinite scuffings of infinite feet behind a double bolted door that's kicked in by the thievin' on a regular basis, an empty fridge and pervasive dinginess defining bone cold poverty.

i rouse her from a stupor, not sleepiness or drugs, but that mental numb cum attending the continual scramblings of those slipping from the edge—the kind of *zombie* ever-continual-unfulfilled-hoping puts one in. and she'll come to the door grabbing some rag up wrapping it around her to keep out the cold i bring with me. and we'll go into her dim funkin' little room and she'll take her spot on the bed and i'll sit in a chair, if there's a chair to sit in, or perch on the corner of the bed near the wall to support my back, or on a crate—whatevah. i'll hand her the bottle then go into my purse and toss her the cigarettes. she'll fire up a smoke get up and scoot out into the kitchen she shares with the other tenant or tenants and grab a couple of cups and we'll share that wine.

she'll start by scoping my vibes. if i'm down she'll ask what's wrong. and i'll respond by telling her to tell me something good. or i might start by saying "what ain't wrong" and then off we go talkin' our talk.

if i've got a little extra coin i might run her round the block or across town to score some skunk. i like it best with young Mexicans cuz they ain't interested in nonsense. they strictly quick business while sometimes a niggah wants to play. the last time i was down i commented on the increased number of young white faces livin' in the neighborhood. it's the cocaine action drawin' them down there—a habit neither one of us can afford to even think about. not that we don't understand the attraction. but what we've got to battle to live is greater than any addiction we can think of. knowin' that keeps us resistant.

near 'bout time for me to go, i'll "loan" her whatevah

i can if i can spare it. which ain't too much too often sometimes only bus fare or phone change. sometimes she'll put the squeeze on me for an extra few cents which i don't like but shine it on understanding the desperation she's driven by. then when we've said all there is to say for the moment we say goodbye. and i backtrack thru the yard smellin' of garbage full of mud and broken concrete car parts old trailers and clutter in general. i nod at her neighbors as i pass. they've come to know me curious at my comings and goings since i'm 'bout the only regular they see. they look at my car and wonder what i'm doin' on their turf unawares i was born and raised there. i try hard not to look too closely into their nosy faces which reflect too familiar a poor circumstance — so much poorer than my own. and surely by most standards i'm poor. but when i leave there i feel all the richer for time spent in her moon glow.

VARIATION ON A FAIRYTALE

she wanted to believe it was nothing
those things couldn't happen to her. she was safe
as a pink newborn in its white bassinet guarded
by Mom & Dad and the keen family cuddlesome canine or
as safe as nuggets and ducats in legendary Fort Knox
as safe as the school marm who loves Sheriff John
as safe as Minnie Mouse as safe as
the pulpit on Easter Sunday as safe as
asexuality. safer than safe

and he let her live with this illusion
promising himself to one day kiss her gently
on each body-brown eye and open her wise to
mundo confundo
he promised, in a grim silence, to protect
her (as long as he was up and able) until that prime time
and then, kindly, slowly he would lower her from
pedestal to ground. together, side-by-side
they'd glory in the sweet sunset of twilight years

but one day the sky shook, parted and fell around them
crushing ever after all fantasy and tiny treasures

when she awoke he had vanished and she had rudely fallen
to earth. she was old, alone and hungry in a harsh hostile
sunlight in the midst of a steamy rain forest
her apron a loin cloth
with no path and no rescue where unusual animals
(not to mention us cannibals)
were gathering were growling

DREAM 1288

walking barefooted thru the streets in a trance, i'm in my thin
lacy worn lavender gown which ill-conceals my brown breasts.
it is sunny and warm
                            my hair is grown long
and processed into a mop of glossy black straw which hangs to
my waist. there's something wand-like in my hand. it's alive.
it's a thick double-headed fleshy yellow-red penis. i work it as
i walk. it expands and contracts with my motions, sometimes
into a putty-like gob
                            i walk thru a business area but draw no
stares as people go about their commerce. i approach a car wash
and begin to walk thru it with the cars. an annoyed Mexican
worker in Dodger blue jacket and baseball cap yells, "hey lady,
get out of the way!" as I step to the
                            side and go around. the
editor-in-chief from Brooklyn appears. she has a note pad in
hand. she wants a survey. several interested passersby stop to
join our discussion as we continue to walk, speaking intelligently
in words i can't decipher. suddenly, the editor

expresses amazement and i snap, "that's reality," turning toward
her so awkwardly i drop the penis. it rolls away across the
blacktop into a pile of newly mown grass. i run over and retrieve
it. it is
                            covered in grass blades. as i hurry home to wash it off
i'm intercepted by a Latin American politico in the lobby of the
library. as the alarm goes off, he hands me a flyer and asks if
i'll please come and do a reading

BURNT

smog and the gray asthmatic noon
the needle's prick for chemistries. no blood
drawn. i'm fresh out

running on ozone

where/what next, shadow boxer?
is it the bell, a horn honk, a scream?
and what is that lump driven over in the street
another hope? another victim of bad weather

my success is on hold

when's the red army marching? you should've used
protection. you should've abstained
you should've brushed your teeth, had a headache
or gotten your degree

(in the dark, descending the jagged steep spiraling
staircase, no end in sight, i look back to find it
vanishing behind me)

 the trumpeter knows/notes music
 as salvation. knows and in blowing, completes
 sacred cycle of do wah wah—rump-jump mojo

 by rote under prod the albino wino scuttles
 bag of pain in hand, sweating the bottle
 on his way to drop the eternal grape and escape
 this sweltering bump on the devil's ass

touched but no feel—smoke inhalation
(thrombosed veins and i'm not even a junky)

lax and numbing beer/semen-like froth
it goes down so arrogant this momentary
swallowing of the cold gold universe

lately of late but not too late???

there's so little happiness in our lives
preoccupied with what we have not

and i'm

all used up. totaled. all gone
lights flashing vacancy. nothin' 'twixt my ears
and less 'tween my thighs

BLACK AGAINST THE NIGHT

what's looked for is many bleeds ago
may never have evah

what you don't see is what you get/an unrepentant
unresplendence of abortions and too-lates
what's dangling status post lynching: the overweight, the
hanky-head, the dead on her feet (aka fat forty and
fucked up)

zero in on the left laughing eyeball, the right orb
bloated, purulent with hate

talk about reparations? hahaha

besides. there ain't cash enuff

the woman who went up in smoke

sometimes a glimpse is caught
and mistaken for a ghost

or doppelgänger

her angry piercing trill could make dead or raise dead
a chill lingering in one's blood

the cold icy corner of a room

her husband testified in court, on television
to everyone

there was no foul play

it was a simple matter of severe aggravated stress
what? — any number of social givens
she was too sensitive to be solid

and went to vapors

WHAT THE BEAST EATS

those yellow portals
glisten in twinight — "surrender"

jaguars mustangs mink
skyscrapers in afternoon sunlight
silhouettes of leafless branches against night shades

it eats sex in the dark and loud music

it eats my peace
and all the dramas in between

2

*the hundred thousand live
in a moment four eternities long*

IN THE KITCHEN MY POTATOES ARE POLEMICAL

english
the scab across my people-tongue
my children in their rooms pick at it

in the refrigerator, an assortment of ideologies
none suit me, flavors faded, colors gone

i read my future in dried coffee rings at the bottom
of my mug/an oracle
bitter in the grind

these days crawl by
my punishment
moms always said i couldn't have my pickle
and eat it too
the petticoat pornographer goes poet

but all i want to write about is me
no one else is doing it

carrots! if i don't get some lettuce soon
i'm gonna do some desperate
drown myself in stew or
shoot myself thru the asparagus
i'm broccolied up to here. i've tomatoed it
the only thing left? pits

new york's words on cunt-eating were rich with the stink
of harlem. she told me i had no accent
and loaned me one
"i'm game for anything," i said, meaning money, not sex

the knife's slipped
i bleed on my potatoes
an added spice to the meal

will anyone notice
if i put my head in the pot?

EL PRESIDENTE

let me tell you it is true

i have been a victim. i was taken in chains to his white house.
i saw the millions dying outside the door and watched as he
paraded thru the streets of the dead seeing nothing. yes, he said
there was no hunger. but the hungry are everywhere sleeping
in doorways, on park benches, in abandoned autos. some are
dying slowly from contamination by chemical or radioactive
waste. some die of diseases caused by their livelihoods — ulcers
and cancers. some die merely of benign neglect. yes — i saw him
and the trick he did with their minds. he reached into a bag
and poured out those dry brittle minds and dropped a handful
of them into a vat of alcohol. they jumped to life as if alive.
i almost shat on myself in fear but kept outwardly cool. those
minds. how horrible. later i made my escape from the white
house to the ghetto. i knew he'd be sending his flunkies after
me — for my mind. he does not want the world to know what
goes on inside these borders — how he thrives on dry and brittle
minds. they will take my mind which is why i send this urgent
warning to you so that you will avoid my impending fate and
the doom of those others. no mind is safe from this eater of minds

as long as we grant him power

TALK ABOUT YOUR DADDY

if i hadda known what kinda man
he really was

he did the best he could. that it wasn't
much wasn't his fault

he was a mean niggah. mean's the best kind
he was so mean the white man feared him
when a white man afraid of somethin' he up and kill it

he was a smooth talkin'
tall walkin'

that niggah ought to be horsewhipped

he died fightin'
for his Civil Rights

you can't judge a man by his color
only by his deeds

sometimes a man gets to believin'
his family can get along bettah without him

sometimes that low down dirty so-and-so
makes me so angry
no tellin' what i'll do

he was the best man
i evah had

the kinda man couldn't give himself to just one woman
that was just the way he was made. took more
than i could give to satisfy his appetite

he wanted me to have a baby by him
so that's why you here

i'm gonna beat that niggah out of you
if it's the last thing i do

he was a powerful man
and then, something seem to take hold of him
and suck out his spirit

i could nevah understand
what made him so evil, why he
did the things he did
try as i might

he asked me if i wanted somethin' sweet
i said yes

he went down
he went down fightin'

all he wanted to do was
get in my panties

he stayed long enough to make you

if i ever see that sorry muthafucka again
it will be too soon

even heaven is segregated. besides
he was always takin' a lot of heat

he was the prettiest black niggah
i evah did see

don't mention that sonofabitch while i'm eatin'

MR. LOPEZ

in german class they used to laugh behind his back
even his best pupils
but i liked to think i was his best pupil
and i didn't laugh

"why do you laugh at him" i once asked
and got no answer

perhaps it was his glasses. they were thick lensed
what we kids called "coke bottles"
or his black hair cut in a quarter-inch butch making
each shiny strand stand at absolute attention
or his crackling white shirts and severe neatness
or his manner. he was tough, daring us to
act up in his presence
like a sergeant "in the gestapo" they smirked
but i saw a sincere man
who loved the german tongue as i was learning
to love it. so what
if his manner was militant, his walk a goose-step
"you've got a crush on him" they said
but that was not so. i respected him as an
excellent teacher
"but how can you" they laughed at me
"it's all so *funny!* what do you think this *is?*"

one day late in the semester
i asked the boy next to me, "what's so funny?
why do they laugh at him all the time"

"because he's a mexican."
i looked at him blankly. "don't you get it?
we're all blacks and here we are in german class
with a mexican for a teacher"

but at that time i was too dense
to get the joke

EMMETT TILL

1

river jordan run red

rainfall panes the bottom acreage — rain
black earth blacker still

blackness seeps in seeps down
the mortal gravity of hate-inspired poverty
Jim Crow nidus

*the alabama the apalachicola the arkansas the aroostook
the altamaha*

killing of 14-year-old
stirs nation. there will be a public wake

works its way underground
scarred landscape veined by rage
sanctified waters flow
go forth

the bighorn the brazos

along roan valley walls blue rapids
wear away rock
flesh current quickly courses thru
the front page news amber fields purple mountains
muddies

*the chattahoochee the cheyenne the chippewa the cimarron
the colorado the columbia the connecticut the cumberland*

waftage

spirit uplifted eyes head heart
imitation of breath chest aheave

that grotesque swim up the styx
level as rainwater culls into its floodplain

the des moines

blood river born

2

ebony robe aflow
swathed hair of the black madonna
bereft of babe

the flint

that hazel eye sees
the woman
she fine mighty fine
she set the sun arising in his thighs

the hudson the humboldt the illinois

and he let go a whistle
a smooth long all-american hallelujah whistle
appreciation. a boy

the james the klamath

but she be a white woman. but he be
a black boy

*the maumee the minnesota the mississippi the missouri
the mohican*

raping her with that hazel eye

the ohio

make some peckerwood pass water mad
make a whole tributary of intolerance

the pearl the pecos the pee dee the penobscot
the north platte the south platte the potomac

vital fluid streaming forth in holy torrents

think about it. go mad go blind
go back to africa go civil rights go go

the red the white the green

run wine

3

silt shallows the slow sojourn seaward

they awakened him from sleep
that early fall morning
they made him dress
they hurried Emmett down to the water's edge

the roanoke

after the deed
they weighted him down
tossed him in
for his violation

the sacramento the salt the san juan the savannah
the smoke

from the deep dank murk of consciousness a birth
oh say do you see the men off
the bank dredging in that
strange jetsam

the tennessee the trinity

a lesson
he had to be taught — crucified (all a nigger
got on his mind) for rape by eye that
wafer-round hazel offender plucked out
they crown him

the wabash

cuz she was white woman virtue and he
be a black boy lust

the yazoo the yellowstone

oh say Emmett Till can you see Emmett Till
crossed over into campground

spill tears
nimbus threatening downpour
sweetwater culls into its soulplain

come forth to carry the dead child home

4

at my mouth forking

autumn 1955, lord!
kidnapped from his family visit
lord!
money road shanty
lord!
his face smashed in
lord! lord!
his body beaten beyond cognition

river mother carries him

laid in state
sovereign at last

that all may witness true majesty
cast eyes upon

murder

the youth's body too light
was weighted down in barbed wire & steel

dumped into the river agape a ripple a wave
(once it was human)

aweigh. awade in water. bloated
baptized

and on that third day awaft
from the mulky arm of the tallahatchie
stretched cross cotton-rich flats
of delta

on that third day
he rose

and was carried forth to that promised land

KOANS

if a lone black man
is arrested
on a dark street
at night
will he end up
in jail?
the hospital prison ward?
or the meat wagon?

*

if a fire starts
in the slums
will the firemen
arrive in time?

*

if a loaded gun
is in the house
will it be used?

*

why does one check
avoid stretching
till the next?

*

does a white man
in a black bar
enjoy his drink?

*

if blacks are only
15% on the outside
why are they 80%
on the inside?

*

what has pink lips
purple gums
and is always happy?

AUGURIES

pied-eyes rhythm sticks & ginger root

a black bird with one red feather

yellow drapes

immediate revelations of unsolicited intimacies

a movie recalled one day
on television the very next

dropsy

an epidemic of spaced-out street people talking
to angels

calls out of name

a black baby succumbed to fire that finds its way to the crib
from the slumlord's faulty fuse box

nystagmus

sudden eruptions on the upper torso which appear
disappear reappear and disappear

forty giant squid beached the death day of
a poet

missing chapters

blank billboards above sunset boulevard

are you watching the skies

ART IN THE COURT OF THE BLUE FAG (9)

i've swallowed something wrong
it takes the vaginal passage to daylight
as i go into a cramped labor more akin to ptomaine
i part my legs (not even having time to get free
of my black nylon panties which burst into shreds)
and give birth

he emerges full grown in chartreuse makeup ragged
as Uncle Sam in gaudy red white and blue tux with
striped slacks mimicking Old Glory, tipping his top hat
of stars (a Broadway musical nightmare) platinum hair
      flagging
grinning like a salacious slick he
high steps as a military band (somewhere in the
backdrop) strikes up the Star Spangled Banner as i
search the ground and my

nappy black pubis for signs of clotting blood
gasping with a second sudden spasm as i expel
a placenta of solid gold

THRU THE GAP

the sensation of falling

itself is not unpleasant. it is the thought of inevitable
trauma on impact that causes my stomach to scramble
throatward. i see my body slammed
against/onto an unyielding darkness. i anticipate
that instant of great relevance after which some
discussion may ensue as to my meaning or lack thereof
not that i'm now of much pertinence. there are no nets
to break my fall. nothing to grab hold to

i plummet

flailing proves wasted effort. better to relax into it
which takes tremendous self control. did i
trip? was i pushed? certainly mine is no accident

my body is in definite downward motion the momentum
stunningly apparent
certain conclusions must be drawn in my effort to accept
the imminent (oh Humpty was it like this?). will my pain
be merely essentialistic? perhaps i will simply burst
into a sweet nothing
                              or will i linger dreadfully after
in searing awareness of my diverse parts, agonizing
a futile reunion to presumed wholeness

AFRICAN SLEEPING SICKNESS

for Anna Halprin

1

four centuries of sleep they say
i've no memory
say they say they i talked quite coherently
i don't remember
four centuries gone

i walk eternal night/the curse of ever-dreaming

sing me a lullaby

2

my father hoists me over his shoulder, holds me
snug to him. i cannot walk
we move thru the sea of stars in blue
i love my father's strength
i love how blue the blue is
and the coolness of stars against my face
he sings me "my blue heaven"

3

i am tied hand and foot
astraddle the gray county hospital bed on the basement floor
my scream smothered in 4x4 adhesive
nothing on but the too short too thin cotton gown
above a naked saffron bulb in socket

nothing else in the ward but empty beds row upon row
and barred windows

i do not know why i'm here or who i am
i see my wounds
they belong to the black child

4

giant green leech-dinosaurs invade the city
superman flies to rescue but weakened by kryptonite
can't stop the havoc
the slug creatures destroy the city, ooze into the Sierras/
along my back into my spinal cord leaving a trail
of upper Jurassic slime

(it gets down to skin and bones. skin/the body's last line
of defense. when awakened the impulse to become — a
cavernous hunger unfillable unsated

                              bones/the minimal elements
                              of survival)

"who am i?"
the physician observes my return to consciousness
the petite white man with sable hair and clark kents
makes note. he is seated in front of a panorama
hills and A-frames sloping to the sea

"who am i," i ask again
"who do you think you are?" he asks
"i'm not myself," i say

5

the encephalopathy of slavery — trauma to racial cortices
resulting in herniated ego/loss of self

rupture of the socio-eco spleen and
intellectual thrombosis

(*terminal*)

sing me rivers the anthem of blue waters the hymn of
genesis

6

lift up your voice and

the tympanic reverberation of orgasmic grunt
                    ejaculatio praecox
traumatized. infected. abrupt behavioral changes
                    the vomitus/love-stuff

he watches me masturbating with the Jamaican dancer
whose hand is up my womb to the elbow
and starts to cry

the weight swells my heart/cardiopulmonary edema
doubled in size it threatens to pop

i ask the doctor why things are so distorted

"we've given you morphine
for the pain of becoming"

7

chills. sing to me fever. sing to me. myalgia. sing to me
delirium. sing to me. fluid filled lungs
i walk eternal night

in the room done in soft maroon warm mahogany amber
        gold
we disrobe to the dom-dom-dom a heady blues suite

216

i pity the man his 4-inch penis
then am horrified as it telescopes upward becoming a
2-quart bottle of Coca-Cola

i talk quite coherently they say

8

fucking in the early dark of evening
mid-stroke he's more interested in being overheard
i go back into my trance as we resume the
6 o'clock news

       the car won't start. the mechanic is drunk
       i can't break his snore. the engine whines sputters
       clunks shutters in the uncanny stillness
       they're coming for me. i've got to escape
       angry, i lash out at the steering wheel, strike
       my somnambulate lover in his chest
       he jumps out of bed yelling
       "what's wrong?"

the curse of ever-dreaming

sing to me, i say. sing to me of rivers

CLOCKING DOLLARS

shell it over
shell it out
smackers crackers nickels & dimes
my weight in bananas

it's all about the moolah

My poverty level steadily climbs. I pay blood for
everything. Open my pages and read my bleed: the essence of
racism is survival; the primary mechanism, economics. The
power to have is the power to do. I, black worker "womon" poet
angelena, disadvantaged first by skin, second by class, third by
sex, fourth by craft (the MSS & juvenilia of pitiably poor poets
pull down greater pissbah posthumously), fifth by regionality.
    Baby—the nights, the days, the hunger. Clean
money writing is a joke. My purse is terminally anemic; the
only cure, Vitamin M as in deep filthy lucre. Unfortunately,
grand theft ain't my style.
    What kind of larceny can a poet perpetrate? What
kind of literary fraud to make it worth my while? Talkin' solid
green, long and mean. Who do I rob?

> *money don't get everythang—it's true*
> *what it don't get i can't use*

I had this thing for greenbacks unsoiled by human
hands. Every two weeks (payday), I went to the bank and asked
for brand new bills. Quickly, the tellers got to know me on sight.
(What could a niggah possibly want with new scratch?) Heads
turned every time I came in. Was I "casin' da joint"? Ultimate-
ly, they could no longer bear the mystery. One woman finally
got up nerve and asked why I wanted new money. I spat forth
my simple passion, lust for the illusion of wealth. The skepticism
reverberated teller-to-teller. They believed I was up to something
crooked.

218

New cabbage must be handled with care; two leaves may cling together as one.

The new simoleans kept getting me in trouble. One day I ordered eleven clams worth of fast food from some Koreans who'd purchased a popular ghetto burger stop. In payment, I snapped a crisp new double sawbuck right before their eyeballs. (Black skin + new money = counterfeit.) They waved their hands in hysterical refusal. All I had were new notes. Outraged, I snatched up hamburgers and French fries and threw them at the ducking dodging Koreans, grabbed my kids and split the scene.

give me five ten fifteen dollars of your love

A man must want you before he'll up cold hard ducats and thus far Congress has been unable to legislate a good stiff dick.

Eager to make my mark on the pop-culture magazine market; idealistically eager to create a rag to counteract the inherently racist imagery of the dominant culture and still turn a profit with cigarette and alcohol ads, I asked him to teach me the ins-and-outs of publishing.

"You want the family jewels, kid." The old Yid picked over his cold potatoes. We always met for lunch at Musso & Frank's Hollywood Grill. I was editing his two hottest soft-porn magazines—bimonthlies. "I ain't givin' you the family jewels," he croaked, forking a spud nugget.

they steal our pain and get rich while we starve

Bleached skin, a nose job and "natural rhythm" are media of exchange = a longer crossover career on the pop music charts + two million per week in royalties. The cash assets of skin: exoticism, suppressed danger, different smells.

Chump change: for the ghetto parasite there's hope in dope—luxury cars, cuban cigars, rubbing noses with movie stars, high-priced likker no need to dicker when the Feds come around to jump your ticker. It's a shame, a disgrace, but they'll tell you to your face: the top's reserved for the White Queen's race.

219

money iszant everythang but
it's way out ahead of whatevah's in second place

Conscious skim for slim volumes of verse has dried up in the new world of mega-corporate publishing birthing the blockbuster (book/movie deal) which is a curious democratization of the world of letters; reversing literary trends blah blah blah (elite busting), forcing the "serious writer" to rely more and more on Academe (don't bite the archives that breed you), Hollywood (become a script rustler), or hang by the good graces of some anonymous endowment cadre. Otherwise, the workforce (be a workhorse) is the only viable alternative. Unless one marries well.

live rich, love easy, die asleep in bed with a smiling corpse

Play literary lotto! Win the critical reviews of your life! Travel to all the important centers of letters in the world! Win a computerized talk-writer, complete with automatic printout, featuring cant, jargon and slang software, your choice of five of fifty foreign languages including Latin and Esperanto — not to mention rhyming lexicon and wordfinder. Yes, you too can be a noted All-American literati!

(Pray worker, pray. Pray your health holds up. Pray your talent survives the hard-drive of corporate sweat. Pray for a New York agent.)

The trial of the contemporary black writer is in earning sufficient dinero by one's writings. If one waits to be courted by the literary establishment à la the fabled Harlem Renaissance one will be cooling one's butt forever. Even if one manages to circumduct that dynamic, Niggah-of-the-Minute syndrome, one will find Academe has its own dastardly limits on black authors (e.g. the month of February) and juggles us interchangeably, without regard to style or gender, since all blacks write about the same thing *ad infinitum,* woojums!

Name: Coleman, Wanda. Normal Retirement Age: 65
Normal retirement Date: December 1, 2011.
Your pension payable at your normal retirement date
under your Mutual of America pension Coverage
is presently estimated to be $38 yearly.

Fear of not making enough — never having been able to make enough. Beastly, it rips at my sleep. In a recent dream, I found some old money, forgotten by a previous employee, in my desk. A Ulysses S. Grant. As I slipped it into my pocket, someone came suddenly upon me. What he said was innocuous; but I couldn't hear it for fear he'd seen me take the money. Worse, had seen the greedy childishness of my need. How I savored it as I palmed it. Worse, my act was witnessed by a white male. And certainly, among *them* I am automatically assumed to be a thief. Immediately, I stormed inside with resentment. They who prevent my socio-economic parity/make it necessary for me to steal, and then, have the unmitigated gumption to accuse me of having stolen (this flesh *stolen* from Africa). Would punish me. And here I am, gone for the okey-doke even in a dream. Waking to realize, my skin is my punishment as much as it is my art . . .

the want that thru the greenbacks drives the power
drives my rage

AMERICAN SONNET

the lurid confessions of an ex-cake junky: "i blew it
all. blimped. i was really stupid. i waited
until i was forty to get hooked on white flour
and powdered sugar"

$$\frac{\text{white greed}}{\text{socio-eco dominance}} \times \frac{\text{black anger}}{\text{socio-eco disparity}} =$$

a)   increased racial tension/polarization
b)   increased criminal activity
c)   sporadic eruptions manifest as mass killings
d)   collapses of longstanding social institutions
e)   the niggerization of the middle class

the blow to his head cracks his skull
he bleeds eighth notes & treble clefs

(sometimes i feel like i'm almost going)

to Chicago, baby do you want to go?

KOANS (2)

how does a nation
repay the debt
of slavery?

*

what danger lies
in a phone number
on the underside
of a matchbook

*

what has a black pelt
smells of musk
and is oft times found
hung from a tree?

*

if you park your car
in a high crime area
will it be there
on your return?

*

if a man has nothing
to do
is he free?

*

when does the punishment
not fit the crime?

*

how does a man
with no heart see?

MOVING TARGET

No, don't label me paranoid.

Nor are mine the symptoms of agoraphobia.

I'm not that tenderheaded.

You know, it's getting so I think twice before leaving the house—uncertain of my return. Sure, in the streets one is always aware of existential danger. But lately the nature of said danger has taken on a more onerous probability—be that possible. This is life-and-death urgency. The goings-on out there drive me to ugly extremes.

I fear my behavior—my short fuse getting shorter—may one day get me very dead. I will explode and be unable to deal properly with some bizarre affront. And my demise won't even make a ripple.

I don't believe in carrying a weapon unless it's to be used. And these days the thought dogs me: *Get some protection.* Every time I go through one of those military surplus stores, the stink of war excites me. I stand at counters for minutes studying the newest fashion in blades and bayonets. And, occasionally, when on my way elsewhere, I'll step briefly into a gun shop to oooh and ahhh at Saturday night specials, stylish pistols and slick automatics. I favor something kept easily concealed. I favor something which will allow the unfortunate asshole who inspires its use to suffer a bit before the final lapse. I prefer something that will fit my palm—a cool second skin, black and intimidating. Yes, that is what I favor.

I fancy it nestled close to me. It and I ready. I imagine the weight of it. Light enough to carry comfortably, heavy enough to comfort me with its immediacy. And its smell. Of course, it must have a smell. The racy odor of exotic oil. The sweaty scent of fear. The aroma of freshly shed blood. And it must have the feel of sumptuous power.

As I move through the streets, by automobile or afoot, I, like most, prefer to keep to myself. Inevitably, eyes find me, define me, and molest me. They are shortly followed by a mouth, or some untoward action that demands I pay attention! Even when in perfect harmony, even when my thoughts are loving, I am not allowed equanimity. My joy inside myself is disrupted, and I must take immediate steps to neutralize the unwanted intrusion. And have no doubt, this saps me — greatly. The energy I could well direct toward a more successful career, is drained from me. Sickeningly. As if some supernatural leech had bled through the pavement and attached itself to my leg, sucking out my life force.

At no time am I the aggressor. Although many seem eager to make that assumption. They judge me by my size, blackness, posture. I seem to inspire fear, hostility, and a nastiness in certain *others*. Or perhaps an imaginary drama in which I need do nothing but passively appear, to be cast in the role of victim. In short, if the gangsters and the racists don't get me, the police will.

I've plenty of examples.

Not long ago, I purchased a television at one of those stores that function as both discount and pharmacy. I was extremely tired, having just left the job. I was so whipped, I didn't even resent the twenty minutes I had to stand at the audio-video counter waiting for assistance. I was the only customer and the clerk didn't feel compelled to hurry to my service. Still, I remained collected as he slowly unlocked the security cabinet, reached in and hefted out the black-and-white portable of my choice. I've always had a preference for black-and-white viewing over color. It leaves more to the imagination. Nowadays they are so inexpensive. I wanted a 12-inch box to fit neatly on a cabinet shelf in my bathroom. It would allow me to relax in the tub and watch a program, or catch the last snatches of a game while showering, before having to leave the house.

I was angelically patient as the clerk (a rosy cheeked Joe College, I surmised) took his time to write up the invoice and ring it into the register. "Will this be cash or charge?"

"Cash," I said pleasantly enough, went into my wallet and handed him two crisp C-Notes. Did the man's eyes bug out? Ah, I thought — he's certain the bills are counterfeit. A nigger with new money must be wrong. Certainly he had been cautioned by management. Hadn't they all? Well if he wants to sell the muthafucka, he'll take them. I looked at the TV. It sported a nice layer of dust and a for-sale sign. I figured he'd take the trouble and 'deed he did.

"Please wait right here, while I make a check." He pressed a button and prayed into the intercom. "Manager at video. Manager at video!"

I stood, smugly patient, idly studying other display items, another six or seven minutes, avoiding the embarrassed clerk's pale gray eyes. Finally the manager appeared, a tweezed up, paunchy little man well into his fifties who was rapidly losing his wavy brown hair. He snatched the bills from Joe College's hands and examined them carefully, placing a loupe to his eye, studying them once more, and then feeling them sensitively with his hand as though he had printed them himself. He grimaced and looked at me, sizing me up. Assessing me as somewhat respectable (probably not the usual type of niggah who passes funny money — he must be expert), he spoke to the clerk, "These are good." And then to me, "It isn't our policy to accept bills of any denomination over fifty dollars. I'm assuming you're unfamiliar with our policy." He pointed to a sign I had failed to see. It was fastened with masking tape to the wooden panel over the display behind the register. From my angle, it had been concealed by the clerk's head. I looked at it and said nothing. The manager sped off without another word as I was finally handed the receipt, my change, and then the television set. It had taken over an hour and my feet were beginning to scream.

The set firmly in my arms, I made my way down the aisle toward the exit. I noticed this particular store had no easy way out from the video department. It required I walk along various shelves of sundries, pass the candy counter and squeeze through the crowded check-out stands, begging pardons as I went. I noticed one check-out counter was closed, a chain blocking it off. I set the television on the counter, removed the chain, slid the set down the counter, put the chain back, picked up the set and made my way to the door. Suddenly I was being accosted by a screeching female employee as black as me, waving her arms frantically.

"Excuse me, but I must check your receipt to see if you've paid for that set!"

"What?"

"That set. You'll have to step over here and let me check it to be sure it's paid for." She was a pretty woman, in her late twenties. I wondered why she hadn't been taught better manners. Surely one black person knows how sensitive the accusation of thievery is to another. Our society treats us as if we were born snatching purses and picking pockets. Guilty of crime from day one.

"Bitch, are you crazy? I bought this not more'n two minutes ago!" I barked and rammed past her. She jumped back to avoid being knocked to the floor. I marched through the door to my car, put the set in the trunk, and drove off angry enough to mow down the first pedestrian to cross against the traffic light while in my path.

An appetizer you say?

The corporate clowns allow me only forty-five minutes for lunch. I try to make good use of this time by furthering some money-making side venture, or running errands which would usually be done over the weekend. A prompt and thrifty person, I consider my time invaluable. I hate to waste it or have it wasted. And I refuse to give my employers one unnecessary minute beyond what has been contracted.

This peculiar day I had opted to run to the post office during lunch. It was only minutes away, and I figured the brisk walk in warm spring air would be lovely and it was. As I neared my destination, I crossed leisurely with the light, *within* the crosswalk. When I got to the other side I noticed two caucasian motorcycle gendarmes studying me with interest. As I caught sight of them, they motioned for me to approach them. Wondering what they could possibly want, I looked around to see if they were motioning to someone else. There was, of course, no one. Curious, but cautious, I went over to them.

"May we see your driver's license?"

"What?"

"Your license, may we see it."

"But why? I'm not driving."

"We suggest you cooperate," said the second cop. There was a menace in his voice that made the hairs rise on the back of my neck. He went into a stance and placed his hands on his hip, one lingering near his billy club, the other near his peacemaker. I quickly went into my wallet and upped the license.

The first cop studied it a bit, turned it over, and then gave it to his partner. They seemed particularly interested in my statistics. "Have you always lived at that address?"

"For the past four or five years."

"You work near here?"

"I'm on my lunch break. Here's my badge," I was wearing it on my lapel. The first cop was closest to me so he leaned forward and examined it briefly, then leaned back against his bike.

"What do you do there?"

"I'm in accounting."

"How long've you been working there?"

"Six, almost seven years." I wanted to ask why I was being questioned, but I had long ago learned, in similar encounters, it's best to speak only when spoken to. And never volunteer information.

"Where are you going?"

"The post office. I need some stamps." Cop number two seemed to find this amusing and sniggered. I didn't dare look at him. It was suddenly too warm and I was starting to sweat. I was also beginning to struggle with my temper.

Cop number one held his arm up and his partner returned the license. He looked at it again. "We're hunting a suspect, and you fit the description — dark skin, black hair, brown eyes, five-eleven, one-hundred-seventy pounds. You don't moonlight, do you?" He smirked. The word moonlight translated as burglarize.

"No." It caught in my throat.

"What'd you say?"

"No officer," I repeated, enunciating clearly, "I don't moonlight."

"That's better." He looked at the second cop who nodded. "Well, it looks like you're not the one we're looking for."

I was relieved.

"But," he continued, "we're going to issue you a little citation here."

"For what, officer?"

"For jaywalking."

"B-butttt," I sputtered. Number two shifted on his

228

hips again, swiveling them in a tight readiness. I clamped my jaws shut.

"Did you have anything more to say about this," the first officer threatened.

"No," I said, swallowing my outrage.

"What did you say?"

"No, officer," I enunciated. "I have nothing more to say."

It took him fifteen minutes to write out the ticket, returning my license with a warning that it would soon require renewal. My lunch hour had vanished along with the cash I'd planned to spend on postage. It would now go to cover the ticket. Feverishly, I returned to the office, ten minutes late, for which I received reprimand. A double whammy.

Speaking of ups and downs, I have the occasion to go out on the town immediately after a hard day's work. At those times I spike up my conservative business attire. Sometimes I will take a complete change of clothes. I had a hot date for dinner and a jazz concert this particular evening. And so I wore silk under my tore-down blue denim suit and vest, my best pair of nines and carried a tam to sport later. After work, I freshened up in the employees' lounge and stylishly donned my tam. I took my briefcase, locked the office, and made for the elevator. It was the tail end of rush hour. One frequently has to wait as the elevator stops at every floor. Impatiently, I paced back and forth. The last worker to vacate, I waited alone. When it finally arrived, the doors zipped open. The car was full of well-heeled white executives on their way to employee parking. They took one look at me and let out a gasp in unison. I was so astonished by their apparent shock *upon seeing me,* I froze to the spot. It took seconds for them to see me clearly. When they recognized me as a member of the firm, they all sighed in relief simultaneously. There was room for one more, but before I could enter, the elevator doors slammed. I remained standing there, wondering. Obviously they thought I was about to highjack the elevator. In their vocabulary one big black niggah plus one black satchel spells terrorist.

I made the concert that night, but somehow I couldn't hear the music.

I was feasting on finely fried catfish at one of my

favorite ghetto juke joints. It wasn't very late, around ten-thirty, as I wiped the grease off my face and fingers. As I made for the door, I was accosted by a youngblood with his palms up. He was clean enough, but raggedy as hell in what remained of coveralls, a T-shirt and sneakers. No socks. He stank of joblessness and snake oil.

"You got money? I need some money. Gimme some money," he demanded in a fierce falsetto.

I looked at him, hid my contempt, and waltzed past him as though he were a ghost (he was). He pursued me. "Come on, I need it — desperate. I wants me some o' dat catfish too, man."

I continued to ignore him, saying nothing, headed straight to my car. Then he made his move. He ran up behind me and grabbed me by my elbow.

"Look, you sonofa—." I never got off my curse. A bunch of nigese low-riders swooped on the parking lot firing hot lead indiscriminately. Both me and the belligerent beggar hit the dirt. There was a sharp crack and we were showered in safety glass. They sped off in a blast of crazed laughter, burning rubber. Youngblood jumped to his feet and, without a word, ran off into the night. I got up and brushed off. Anxiously, I turned to get into my car. The windshield was shattered. There was a bullet hole in the right rear just *above* (thank somebody) the gas tank.

Enough of this prolonged whine? Insufficient evidence? Consider all the usual bullshit one goes through in life, and then multiply. These incidents, taken separately, over months, might prove annoying, but certainly one should be able to cope. But they, and the like, happen to me two, three, four times *per day*. If not more. I am constantly reminded that I am who I am. Dutch chocolate in a cherry-vanilla world.

I try to be tolerant. I try to appreciate the socio-economic-historical ramifications — as they say on the six o'clock news. I try to keep my best foot forward and continually tug at my bootstraps. I coach myself daily, insisting I am above it all. I'm not.

Please somebody, no more. I'm sick of this abuse. It's bleeding me dry. It's killin'. I've got to do something other than complain. I must get some protection.

There are two alternatives: guns or money. Money protects in the distance one can buy; another neighborhood, bodies-for-hire to fend off the world, while one is cloistered in luxury. I'm white collar poor, so my option is obvious. A hand gun will fit nicely within my limited budget.

Yes. It's a good decision. The right decision. Already I feel like the human being this world keeps saying I'm not — full of indignation and determination.

I'm finished paying dues.

I'm through with being taxed for my birthright.

Some sonofabitch is gonna pay for this shit.

Next time.

PROVE IT WHY DON'T YOU

fox in the hen house shoo fox shoo

who say who suffer most? colored folk say
there's little cultural guilt & less national empathy
(one is always used to one's own stink)
about so-called misery, present the irrefutable
evidence. take it skip-to-my-loo. all have crosses to bear
except some have great big wooden ones with splinters
and termites and some got little 24K gold diamond studded
crosses and some are born nailed to theirs and others
got to make 'em themselves and still others
buy theirs at the finest roodmakers. show the wound
let's touch to see if it hollers
squeeze it and let the pus owl-eye to the surface

now, darlin', who co-opted your form and
coyoted your content?

but seriously—birds do sing
and telephones ring-a-ling

as for slavery
don't come crying about what's been stolen
from you. besides

acts of oppression are sexy and
good hard thangs grow in tight wet places

BONES OF CONTENTION

for Lois, deceased

he described you as a cracker battle axe
but the woman i met was thin and haint-like

i spoke to you as little as one can speak
to an in-law and get along
as did you
we never called one another by name
converse for sake of function
biding, tolerant

whenever the three of us sat down together
he preached his gospel of civil rights
you silent, as was i
wishing he would let us be—each in her own distance

and as the social pressures of our miscegenation
ate away love
i tried to make him understand
the dangers

the whip has bitten into the back of the slave
clean thru to the heart

sing dixie
wave the stars & bars

our marriage decomposed into a gangrenous animosity
no understanding—black or white

six years after divorce he called long distance
you were dying of colon cancer
your last wish
to see your grandchildren

he begged me to send the kids

i said no

and he will never understand

SOME OF US

are found hanging
from tree limbs or in jail cells
embraced by bed sheets

some of us are found frozen over
by amphetamines, opiates and/or alcohol
drowned in the unsavory substance of life's
denied possibilities

some of us are strangled by The Law
beaten. clubbed. shot
mistaken for the criminal we should be
for the crime they fear we may someday commit

some of us go scrambling
frantically, futilely, for the last-minute luck
it is thought will catapult us out of
tarry despair

some of us go slowly, quietly
bled alabaster
by the circumstance of skin — lost
boxers of shadow, exhausted and stilled by
the cobwebs of abstractions

some of us die by assassination
for having spoken the unpopular black of truth
too long too loudly to too many

some of us are aborted
by malnutrition of spirit/body, trying to keep up
the mechanical intensity
survival in Amerikkka demands
                              suicided

some of us die humanely
at the will of the state
in a drugged sleep

none of us die laughing

UNFINISHED GHOST STORY

i pushed my fingers thru Clive's scrotum and wiggled them around. he felt no pain and did not complain. his face was scrunched up in concentrated pleasure as he pumped away on top of me.

i turned my face to my right and strained to peep at my fingers. they were perfectly clean. i sniffed for some detail of scent. there was none. and while i felt little beyond a vague discomfort he was groaning ecstatically in the throes of orgasm.

he rose abruptly and reached for the towel on the night table.

"that was fucking incredible. how was it for you?"

"equally incredible," i lied.

he smiled so broadly and so sincerely i regretted having to lie. i had no choice.

"let's shower then have breakfast somewhere," he chirped.

"cool with me."

all i wanted was a hot croissant. i buttered it lavishly but could only pick at it over my coffee.

"something's wrong, Regina. i can feel it."

"i'm glad you can."

"what's that supposed to mean?"

"i'm not feeling well . . . is all."

"why didn't you say so? i could've waited."

"i don't mean sex. i—i'm not sure what's come over me. the world doesn't seem to have much substance anymore."

"that's overstating it. one need only take a look at the evening news to ascertain that much."

"that's not quite what i mean."

i brooded for too pregnant a second, bursting with my truth, debating on telling him. i hadn't the nerve or the energy.

"it's nothing, Clive, i guess—bad digestion, as they say in the gothics. i can't eat this thing."

"well, we can't let good French pastry go to waste, now can we?" he said and lifted it from my saucer.

LATE ONE NIGHT

two weeks before her obituary appeared i was sitting
in the dark round back of the Parisian room debating
on whether or no to go in and catch her show or go home
sit alone stewing in mah-man-of-woe-don't-want-no-mo
when the side door back of the bar-be-que joint opened
up and out steps this long tall woman in a straw stetson
gray blouse and slacks and cowboy boots carrying a
brown paper bag i recognize Big Mama Thornton i figure
she's totin' ribs in red sauce and it makes me hungry
it's been over fifteen years since i caught her act at a
San Francisco blues joint and she's lost a lot of weight
all the fat round jelly gone (mis'ry slim a legend to
a whisper, i thinks) and she sees me watching her and
nods a sistuhly hello i nod back and start to speak
but think bettah not considering my do-evil mood may
embarrass myself and i get out and go in to enjoy her
show but not before i cop some of them ribs

■

he tells me there will be nothing
to write about in this life with him
no stories for the general public
no fresh fuel
i will be smothered in the dull dependability of love
the excitement of the outside world
will be squelched
nothing for the confessional
nothing to burn

THE FIRST DAY OF SPRING 1985

polemic for Tim & Kathy Joyce

lust for liberty sprouts seventeen dead

blackest black South Africa

camera action: blood & shoes. (remember the mountains of
      shoes?)
the commemoration of sixty-nine slain in Sharpeville
the militia swarms down on the marchers the township
and disenfranchised *children* become
"angry bands of roving youths" throwing rocks and epithets
at billy clubs automatic machine guns tanks cannon
      H-bombs

sanctioned slaughter

two cops transform a protestor's head into mulch on the
6 o'clock news

    within minutes the patriarch of America II
    appears via satellite
    will he increase his "hard-line" policy
    toward South Africa?

    no.
    the situation (apartheid) is deplored by all
    but these *were* rioters
    and some of the police who stopped the violence
    were *black*

    video pornography
    the slave is blamed for slavery
    he whitewashes and soft-pedals
    genocide

i am out of my senses — splib splob

238

home of the lynch mob
land of the vigilante

World War III is now taking place — an economic holocaust

who remembers Mary Smokes?
who remembers Wounded Knee?
who remembers The Night of the Long Knives?
                    Kent State? Jackson State? Attica?
                    The Greensboro Five?
                    Geronimo?

(in 1819 i was stoned to death in the streets of Philadelphia
                    by three white women. who am i?)

                              *

hello from months later

i am fighting to stay in the classroom —
no open minds

i am teaching Lord of the Flies
telling the youths about Manson &
Jim Jones' temple of doom
Sympathy For The Devil / Altamont
Hell's Angels

and this girl looks up to me and says
"are you making this up?"

who remembers the tongue of the man who has no tongue

3

*the cry of forever yearning can be heard
in the heart of a people*

CURRENT EVENTS

the welcoming committee
was concerned. they marched on city hall
protesting the hospices. a spokeswoman
stated they do not want death
in their neighborhood

certain victims have been noted
to indulge in bizarre behavior. a few
have bitten policemen

secular celibacy and "moling in" (non-denominational)
have become recent trends

Tim the young blond waiter at the Vine St.
knew we were poets who hung for the jazz. he always
gave us the best tables. we missed him when he left
assuming he'd gone on to a better gig. later we
found out he'd died of the virus

following the sudden death of her young adult child
one mother complained of weird behavior
on the part of neighbors church members and
long time friends

there's a hole in France where the
naked Jani dance

THE EDUCATIONAL LAB COUNSELOR

our son's got math problems. his stepdad my
lover goes to the school to check it out. he
gives me a report on Mr. So-and-So. the man is a
uranian, very low profile, helpful and nice enough
but doesn't look well and is rather thin for a man
his size. but he's promised to assist our son as much
as possible

a few weeks later our son brings home a bad math
report. we jam him. hasn't Mr. So-and-So been
helping? he tells us the man's been out sick. we
exchange a look and say nothing. so many uranians are
falling terminally ill these days. we decide we'll
have to coach him ourselves. more time to sacrifice

the next day my husband his stepdad calls the school to
ask about Mr. So-and-So. he's on indefinite medical leave
with something serious though no one will volunteer what
that is. odd for so young a man. we suspect he has the
virus and the school is keeping mum to avoid hysteria
among parents

of course we may be wrong

A LATE 80s PARTY

the dude who opens the door is as thin as
a dollar bill standing on its side
he looks like he has the virus
i shake his hand hoping i have no cuts or
open sores. the hostess cheerily assures me
her roomy is a nice midwestern guy even though
they never had sex. i'm
reminded of time served on the TB ward
at county. all those skeletons walking
around gave me a permanent hanker for
meat on the bone. tonight
very few people show so i linger to
pay friendship dues and do the party. it's
hard times. it's been well over twenty years
since i've made a set where the main event's
frankfurters and potato chips. not to
mention there's only "ade kool"
on the bar. there are two or three joints floating
around. i get grimly happy trying to get in
the spirit with some insignificant
chit-chat then watch a video trying hard not to
watch the clock. when my meter runs out i
hurry home to soak my hands in betadine wash
making note that sharing smokes these days is
really not where it's at

CHANCE MUSIC

cultural felo-de-se

random sounds/explorations of interiors or exteriors
evoking redefining illuminating

risk being habit which insures being
in the world

(statistically conductors & novelists live longer
than poets & jazz musicians) the argument for
peer recognition beyond marketing factors:

he hastily unpacks books gifts keepsakes
"please don't lose the receipts," i chirp
"the minute we get home you start," he snaps

supporting what is easily observed in the rash
on my backside (karmic noodlings)

it's getting old
it's got a powerful rank
it's growing whiskers
it's droppin' off the bone
it's the oldest piss in the pot

my continued strive to achieve solidity
substance synonymous with salability (what makes a black
            man
pariah makes the white man rich)

AUGURIES (2)

rose hips ginseng dandelion & dill

a white cat perched on a window sill

gray pallor

existence marred by extremes of ambivalence

a woman in the downs
compulsively peeling Spanish onions

borborygmi

an interrupted trail of hooves along the soft shoulder
of a freeway on-ramp

dander up

the burial of a black child crushed to death under the
weight of his mother

hyperpnea

an obsession for light accompanied by the
uncontrolled rolling of Rs

born the year of the bikini

deadbolts on broom closets

wind-blown lavender toile curtains against a
red pacific

it is going to storm

■

he told me his mother tickled him
in his sleep
i did not understand
until it was too late
to call the authorities

AUGURIES (3)

reefer champagne C-notes & mellow

a dark moody round midnight

blue gardenias

the wisdom of the alto sax fallen to temporal blues

a sultry sequined torch
burning against the abyss

bleak bebop sheebop

take the A train/take 5/after hours — eighths
of that

shades at night

a black man puts a magnum to the head of his infant
daughter and is wasted by s.w.a.t.

whatchewknow daddio

ebony cats with vine lives reeds and the
sweet stroke'n slide

an avenue ace of thorns nailed while with another's
womon

shades of drang

the wistful whistler up the avenue

johnny hartman johnny hartman

HOW DOES IT HURT

tell me, how does it hurt
let me heal your wound
tell me, how does it hurt
i can heal it soon
i have any number of cures
many ways to improve
so tell me, how does it hurt

tell me, where does it hurt
let me ease your pain
tell me, where does it hurt
what have you to gain
hiding all your feelings inside
only makes it worse
so tell me, where does it hurt

refrain: pain. you can't avoid it
pain. can make you grow
love. you must embrace it
if love you want to know

show me, where does it hurt
let me ease your ache
show me, where does it hurt
there's so much at stake
hiding all your troubles from me
only makes it worse
show me, where does it hurt

SOMETHING IN MY THROAT

eventually it will cause trouble
experts say
they will operate and excise it
they refuse to tell me what it is
i am angry about that
but am convinced they're telling the truth
i have no way to be sure — no means
to vital information
if i ask too many questions
they will
label me an agitant

on one hand i must open my mouth
and on the other
keep it shut

THE SKULLCAP

there's a leak in the bathroom in the pipes in the wall. he cleans
out the mess beneath the sink and puts down newspaper to ab-
sorb water dripping into the cabinet and to the floor. the manager
will be calling the plumber. it's cold, rainy and it's snowed in
this region for the first time in twenty-odd years

next morning i notice the wine-colored yarmulke curled up on
top of the glass canisters in the kitchen. i remember it belongs
to the landlady's grandson. he rented us this little hole. i recall
those strange brown eyes of his which glimmered intensely with
cunning as though he were putting one over on us. i leave it

the next evening he notices the yarmulke, picks it up and asks
about it. "it belongs to what's his name, you know." he starts
to throw it away but it's pretty, tightly knitted with a band of
white trim woven thru the wine. "i think i'll keep it," he says,
"and put it in a collage"

her grandson left for Israel after a friend took his room upstairs
out back. he used to be the lover of the man who died here of
the virus. i start to remind him but stop because the kids are
standing nearby and can overhear our conversation as i prepare
dinner

the next morning he calls me at work. the plumber says it's going
to be expensive to repair the pipes. he called the landlady to
get her okay on the price. out of courtesy he asked about her
grandson and she tells him he died a month ago in Israel. it
was a slow painful death, she says but does not mention the cause

SUNDAY MORNING STROLL

it's one of those days this region's famed for, crisp obscenely clear blue sky, billowy cumuli, greener greenery, storybook homes — everything looks brand new. we take the kids out for pancakes, waffles and eggs. afterwards, we take a slow lengthy walk from the restaurant back to the car parked at the top of a hill. as we walk the hill, ahead of us a blond man skinnies out of his apartment. we watch him. he has on light blue denims and matching sweater. his pants are as small as they come for men and he bags in them. a bag of bones. he goes to his car, gets something small he's forgotten, and conceals it in his hand. as he crosses before us again i look at his face. he has a bad complexion but no virus-related tumors. he hurries back inside as we stare after him. in Africa, i think, it's called the slim disease. my man and i make a noise simultaneously. he turns to me and says, softly, "aren't we lucky" and i agree with a nod. we say that a lot lately, like a prayer

HOMAGE TO AN OLD WHITE LADY GROWN ILL

she had it all. she wants it back

partial paralysis confines her to the double-railed
hospital bed. a stainless steel triangular bar is braced
above it so she may do lifts and shifts in position
to prevent bed sores. her skin luminously thin betraying
blue vessels and fierce bone

this niggerization of the body (oh once so desired
those tits & ass) has awakened in her a virgin rage
not age but infirmity and the indignities that accompany
a loss in bowel & bladder control which inspires
an outlandish militancy

storming against the white sheets suggestive of her
pending ghostly state, she bemoans this greedy nation
the presidents she helped empower, the causes she disdained
now, herself, ranked among the needy & discarded

her keen mind impaled and wiggling
on the spit of feckless vision and misdirected faith

she had it all. she wants it back

she would pit her mouth against the void
balloon it with hot breathy tirades of
indignation. she would incise it like a pussy furunculus
drain and cleanse it in alcohol, apply cotton and gauze

from her wheelchair, armed with vitriol, in ragged chevrons
she would lead an embittered charge to overthrow
the arrogant, the richly unconcerned, the mobsters
and die embattled trusting victory to the innocent, the
humble, the caring, the true

she would gather her army from the legions of
the drugged the numb and the mad — those who never lived

in her neighborhood, the foreign to prosperity who never
crossed the borders of her sheltered well-educated youth
or disturbed her appetite for the classics with
whines of injustice

now she'd turn on her own culture
wring its neck, cut and gut it
to feed the bloodthirsty in whom
she sees herself

OBITUARIES

i always read them looking for cause
noting official biographers refuse to speak ill
(especially if it's venereal) until recently. all those
dropping dead of complaints related to the virus
exacerbated, the public's told, by health abusive
life-styles, get their business put in the streets

this white man in his early 30s came into the doctor's office
one day. he was blond, a perfect well-muscled surfer type.
it was discovered he was rotting inside out. he didn't
have the virus. devout christians he and his wife
married as virgins and swore to faith. he'd been
a health food buff for life. raised on it. never ate
junk food. never drank. never smoked. never did
drugs. got proper sleep. lived in remarkable
disciplined goodness. he felt betrayed by God/his body

most all the ones under forty-five've died
of it

a blonde woman i know opines the virus is the best thing
that's happened to marriageable females
since the veil

THE DEATH OF A FRIEND

what he died of

will be published in capital letters
indictment more than cause

this time they will spell his name in full
and correctly
a small photo of him smiling flatly will draw eyes
of the empathetic (taken prior to prolonged period of
being jaded and cyanotic)

he was too young, of course, but then
aren't they always too young
what he could've given the world
what he could've . . .

and there will be a memorial testimony
ashes to urn

flowers perhaps

his color, which may have been significant
is no longer relevant. his lovers
he she they

pray

DÉJÀ VÉCU

I haunt myself as though I'm my own ghost. And that's funny because I'm certainly alive, existent. I feel myself breathing in and out at this exact moment. Deeply inhaling, exhaling, here in this night, in my bed.

I know I'm alive, laying here, trying to figure it out. If, obviously, I'm alive, why don't I feel like it? No, that's not quite the question. If I'm alive, why am I not living? That's it. I'm surviving, not living. And this is news to me.

I have name, shape, definition. Each morning when I shower water rushes against my breasts and down my thighs, speaking life. When I look in the mirror, there I am. About the house there are dirty dishes to wash. I wash them. I dust. I move the furniture. I have a job to go to and take the bus to get there. I have a desk at which to sit. People see me going about and doing things as assigned. I'm spoken to, if, sometimes, only vaguely, but spoken to, certainly. I feel air give way as I move through it. I feel objects in my hands when I pick them up. A book, say. A bottle as I pour a glass of wine. When I drink the wine it quickly goes to my head, arousing giddiness. When I take a draw on a cigarette, the heat warms my fingers. When I inhale the smoke there's a tiny stinging sensation deep in my chest. When I exhale, the smoke makes its way slowly, visibly toward the ceiling. All of this seems ample evidence.

I have periodic interaction with another, a gentleman friend I've known for some time. He takes me out to dinner, a movie, to dance. And afterwards, at my apartment, his, or perhaps in a motel room, we touch. Our sexual intimacy reassures me. His erection is documentation and his ejaculation, validation.

Yet somehow all this is inadequate diagnosis of anything, particularly proof of my existence. Anyone else could do these things as well. There is no need for me, specifically, to do them. I'm haunted by this impression that if I stop doing them, no significant change will take place. Because none of what I bring about produces important enough effects. Not for me, anyone, the world. Yet I do these apparently non-vital things to survive. To receive my biweekly income. Thus I'm alive not living. Eating, breathing, sleeping with occasional sexual release. The things done. The job. The life. But all somehow unimportant.

I haven't always felt this way. Quite recently, my life seemed to have had possibilities. And then, one day, I met a tattered woman in the streets. It was on this first encounter that I became obsessed with the question of being.

I was on a bus headed west. I had an appointment and was late. These goddamned buses are infuriating during rush hour. The drivers are such lazy assholes. Forget the scheduling, they never stick to it. A bus is supposed to stop every few designated minutes at a given stop during a given time of day. If they don't feel like stopping they'll drive past, leaving you standing there, helpless, in a hissy as they smugly cruise by. Such behavior might be justified when buses are full, people jammed back to front. But half the time they're empty and behind schedule, and they know there's another bus minutes behind them. And they've probably had a shitty day, knowing the kinds of crazies who are likely to come on board. But it's their job for which they're paid. They're supposed to stop. Arbitrarily they don't which frequently happens when I'm the only one waiting at a stop. And I don't know who or what to blame. Their circumstance or mine. If the bus driver isn't black, I accuse him or her of being racist. But if black, I simply dismiss him or her as bourgeois, thinking they're better than I because if I were of any substance I wouldn't be taking buses. I'd have a car, even a piece of a car, like most successful or semi-successful people in this city. Only domestics, the destitute, students, the elderly, the crazed, and the auto-phobic take the bus. And among those, very few white males.

When she got on the bus I couldn't help but notice her. She looked like me only decades older. There were differences, certainly, but surface and minor. Her skin was a chocolate brown identical to mine, but blotched by big patches of a ghastly pinkish-white discoloration, as well as patches of dirt caking her skin. She had some sort of systemic malady, the kind shockingly visual when involving black skin. It looked as though her skin was turning white under pressure — some kind of stunning vitiligo.

I'm not displeased with my color. I like being chocolate brown. I'd never ever stoop to bleaching my skin or changing any of my grossly negroid features. I like the way I look, no matter what others think—even the "healthy" fat dimpling my buttocks. And this woman looked like me only heftier, and, of course, those skin changes, and she had overgrown buttocks the way I imagine mine will look in twenty or thirty years. One of those well-rounded *sistuhs*. And she had my legs, the sacred legs of the stork, straight and calfless, bowing slightly outward, leading up to fatty knees and then ballooning into enormous soft thighs large enough to cradle an entire civilization. Many's the man who's told me the best kind of pussy may be found between those kinds of legs. Our legs.

And her stomach, it's much bigger than mine. I still have some flatness. I don't drink much, enough to be social. Alcohol doesn't sit well with me. Her stomach is huge and beery almost as if she's pregnant. I've seen men and women like that, all kinds, all colors, wearing the boozy tire of self-hate around their middle. Surely she's like many of these street people, an alcoholic or wino.

Once I saw a woman walking down a hallway. She had one of those sheep-dog hair styles which made it difficult to tell her front from her back. It took me a few moments to realize she was walking toward me instead of away from me. She had tiny breasts and a strange, overly large stomach. She was too mature to be pregnant. Her belly hung low like an obese rear end, poked out, with that fleshy inverted extradoses at the crack. When she walked past me, I turned around and followed her a little ways to be sure I was seeing what I was seeing. Once certain, I was overcome with pity for the woman, wondering what could have caused her ugly condition. As I studied her, she felt my thoughts and turned to look. Her eyes revealed pain and to avoid it, I pretended to look beyond her, down the corridor at some other destination. She turned quickly and went about her business and I went back to minding mine.

The tattered woman isn't quite that bad, although well on her way. Otherwise, she is rather pleasant-looking in spite of her uncleanliness and obesity. She is tall, about my height at five-eight. Her hair is a wild bush of tangled kinks without care or design, so lengthy they halo her head and shoulders.

260

She dresses in all kinds of paper held to her body by thick brown string. Some of it cotton wadding, some of it newsprint, most of it butcher paper. In places she reinforced it with disposable plastic trash bags. That afternoon she got on the bus like that, with her arms, like aimless brown legs of pork, exposed, all that flesh wobbling. And her stiff brown legs poked out from under her trashified "dress," spotted chocolate and pink-white. Her eyes searched the aisle for a seat, and as she passed me, chills went through me, head to feet.

I was looking at myself.

I've begun to see this woman two or three times per week. Obviously, she's not following me. Perhaps I'm following her. We "live" in the same community. She causes me that bizarre sensation of chills each time I set eyes on her. It's as though I become transported through time, watching the scenario I've written, wondering how I could come to this. I find myself sitting for hours contemplating what might lead me to such desolation. What ignorance, what trauma? I have no answer.

I work hard. I get up every day and get to my job. I'm responsible. I pay my bills. As mentioned, I have a pleasant social life. There's nothing abnormal about me. I have average abilities and average aspirations. I'm not completely satisfied with my job, but it has its compensations. And being independent, these days, is nothing extraordinary for an urbane black woman of my age and income bracket. There's nothing unusual about me. I'm patriotic and I believe in God. I'm a modest reader and manage to keep up with the styles, if only barely.

And yet, there she is.

It's as though she's some kind of remark. Some kind of comment on my state of being. Some kind of mockery. Her existence is something I'm both fascinated by and resentful of. And while I've spotted her from my bus seat window many times, seen her on street corners, begging handouts, plucking savories from public waste cans, whenever I've come close enough to speak to her, I can't. My mouth remains clamped shut as I stare at her then hurry off.

Besides, what would I say to her. Acknowledge kinship? Accuse her of following me? And if she is somehow truly myself, wouldn't talking to myself be further indictment of some sort? Doesn't that sound sick? I've given it a good deal of thought. This feeling has come up on me only quite recently, since seeing this street woman, this filthy apparition who jumps out at me suddenly from park benches and alleyways. Inevitably, when I'm walking past closed shops, looking in windows, I catch sight of her snoring like a banshee in a darkened doorway. And lately, I've begun to wonder if she's haunting me or if I'm haunting her.

Again, I was on a bus headed west. In this city the best money opportunities are on the west and northwest sides of town, and I was hoping to improve my situation with a better paying job. I had an interview. I believe in promptness and feel it important to be on time, if not a few minutes early. But there is no way for me to possibly be punctual with the buses running so capriciously unless I plan extremely carefully.

My problem was how to get to the new job interview by six o'clock. I couldn't leave my job early without arousing suspicions of my supervisor; besides, being wedded to the time clock, I had established a pattern of punching out religiously at five. And I had no desire to risk losing one job before having secured another.

To further embellish my quandary, it was necessary to take two buses, the first one south and second west. The nearest bus stop south was a five minute walk from the building in which I worked. I had sufficient opportunity to plot my every stop short of a dead run. According to the schedule, the bus I needed was due at the stop at exactly four-fifty. Therefore, I needed to clock out fifteen minutes early in order to make my interview on time. A second southbound bus arrived at ten minutes after five, but taking it would make me disastrously late, ruining my chances, and making me ten minutes shy of catching the westbound bus which had a slower schedule at fifteen to twenty minutes and intersected with the southbounder of choice at exactly five-fifteen, leaving forty-five minutes in which to make my appointment exactly forty-five minutes away. As unclearly as I may detail it, two things were vital: leaving the job fifteen minutes early and making the five-fifteen westbound bus.

I was in for some luck that morning coffee break when one of my co-workers, another sistuh, pulled me aside, confidentially, as I was leaving the employees' restroom. She needed a favor and asked if I'd clock her out the next day so she could make her beauty parlor appointment on time. I agreed in exchange for her doing the same for me that very evening. Thus we became co-conspirators, knowing that to clock out a fellow co-worker was strictly against corporate "law."

This incident started my adrenaline rushing.

I made my getaway and the bus stop on the dot. Looking north I could see the bus two blocks away. As it approached, I had the sickening realization that the driver was not braking to a halt. He was going to bypass me. And he did, looking out at me, grinning.

Livid, I stood watching it sluggishly cruise off. In a panic, I stuck out my thumb to hitchhike, determined I would show that negro clown my ass. Piqued by the rage beneath my modest front office appearance, a Japanese gentleman spotted me and pulled over to the curb. As I climbed in, I sensed his interest in picking me up was to establish a sexual liaison. I flatly told him I had to catch the bus that had just passed, leaving me stranded. I neutralized his lust by offering him a couple of dollars to take me to the juncture. Amused, he refused my money but was game for the race and took off, maneuvering expertly through traffic. We sped along in dense silence, my neck craned forward in anticipation as I clutched my purse, my pressed hair bouncing with the jostling motion of his stylish little economy class pseudo-sports car.

"There's that sonofabitch!" I giggled madly when we caught up with the bus. He muttered words lost to me in my fever as I shouted, "Pass him! Pass him up! Now, yes, now."

The Japanese gentleman seemed to thoroughly enjoy our little jaunt as he whipped in front of the bus. When we neared the juncture I shouted, "There! There! Pull over and let me out!" He smiled and did as asked. I scrambled out, thanking him, and curtly shook his hand for a chase well accomplished. His head bobbed in broad laughter as he drove off.

There came the bus. I stood ready, grinning viciously as it curbed to a stop. As the doors opened for passengers to disembark, the driver saw me, recognized me and gasped. I gave him "the finger," indicating he was to go fuck himself, took my dignity and marched across the street to catch the approaching westbounder, savoring my victory. As it arrived, I stepped aboard, went into my coin purse and plucked out the exact change. As I dropped it into the fare box, I casually asked the driver if she'd call my stop as we approached it. She said nothing but stared straight ahead as if I hadn't spoken. She was a robust sistuh, a little taller and heavier than I with round features, honey-colored skin and short curly ginger hair.

I repeated myself and she glared at me, uglied up her face and stated she'd never heard of the street. Thrown by her nastiness, I realized she had to know the stop since it was on her daily route. Cockily I said, "Well, fuck you too," and found myself a seat in the back.

As the bus traveled further west, the complexion of the passengers lightened until we were the only two blacks present — me and the driver. The others were elderly whites and a few hispanic domestics.

When the bus crossed the major intersection near my stop, I began watching the side streets. As my stop approached I rang the buzzer and stood at the rear exit. The bus did not slow down. I rang the buzzer repeatedly. Still that bitch of a driver ignored me. I began cursing her loudly. I raced to the front to somehow make her stop before the bus went too far for me to comfortably walk back in time to keep my appointment. Alerted, the passengers watched us.

At her station I looked at the control panel and realized the break switch was out of my angry grasp. I'd have to reach over her to get to it. She wasn't going to let that happen. She looked up into my face with a haughty grin and I spat into it. Shocked and incensed, she slammed on the brakes and rose to confront me. I was game.

She threw a punch with her left hand and I short-stopped it by grabbing her wrist with my right and holding it, grabbing at her hair with my left to try and snatch out a few of those ginger curls. Her whole scalp rose in the air with my tug and the passengers gasped. She was wearing a wig. Beneath it, her natural hair was criss-crossed by teensy kinks of honey brown hair parted into neat rows of squares. Within the center of each little square was a patch of hair, knotted and rubber-banded into neat clove-like nubbins. Her head looked like an over-baked ham.

Greatly embarrassed, she pushed me backward toward the little stairwell at the front exit. I clutched the side railing and regained my balance, avoiding a fall backwards. She tried to dislodge me with one hand while retrieving her wig with the other. She threw the wig behind her seat to keep my hands off it. An overly busty woman, her chest strained at the buttons of her drab gray driver's uniform as we exchanged blows. My eyes betrayed my intention to rip open her shirt and expose her bosom to public scrutiny. Reading me, she hissed, stepped back abruptly, pulled the lever opening the door, and shoved me backwards through it.

I went crashing on my skirted behind onto the pavement. The door snapped shut and within seconds the bus was racing off west along the boulevard.

To the amused amazement of passersby I sat for a minute, checking for damage. I was unhurt. I didn't even have a run in my stockings.

And then there it was. This big meaty chocolate hand extended out to me. It was her — the derelict. She was smiling kindly, her eyes glittering with a fierceness that must've matched my own. I took her hand and got to my feet as she half lifted me with her strong forearm. I was nearly overcome by the smell of things rotting. I snatched my hand away and busied myself brushing off my skirt. She stood there breathing heavily, frowning, concerned. I went into my purse for a dollar, but she snubbed it, said nothing, rolled her eyes at me and waddled away. As I hurried off to my interview, I smelled my hand where she had touched me but there was no fragrance out of the ordinary.

That is the only time we've made direct contact, although we've come close enough on subsequent meetings.

When, outside, in the streets, I find myself in a state of acute unrest, I suddenly look up, around, or about and see that tattered woman loping up the avenue or stepping out of an alleyway. Our eyes always meet.

I've become preoccupied by her. I've even worked out elaborate dialogues between us. I've also envisioned violence, seen myself attacking her, beating her senseless, angered she's allowed herself to sink so low, decrying her subhuman status. Doesn't she know what she looks like? Smells like? Does she ever take a bath? Why doesn't she lock herself up somewhere? Out of my sight, particularly. Was she ever married? Was it his fault? Doesn't she miss the company of men? Does she ever give herself to those foul homeless male wrecks who also haunt the streets? The speculation sends me reeling with disgust.

What tragedy has brought her to this? She could be mentally ill. But somehow I know she's not. I suspect her thoughts are as lucid as my own. I seem to hear them, as if they're my thoughts. But of course they aren't. They're hers. Yet I'm somehow, spookily, made privy to them. And this is dreadful, because I'm certainly not her alter-ego, nor is she mine. We have nothing to do with one another. Yet somehow we're linked. As surely as dust rises and settles.

More frightening is my certainty that there was no disrupture to bring about her current state. No death or disaster, but mere social dissipation—a happenstance so gradual she had no sense of progress, no awareness of danger, no warning. One day she found herself as she is, homelessly wandering the streets, scratching out sustenance among like others, unwanted and unemployed.

Daily, I monitor my life for any possible clue, constantly detecting. I sense the answers are here with me in my life as I hamster about. And that too frightens me. It's become a question of identity. Who I am distinct from some imagined future me. Or the self I see reflected in her existence—that tattered woman. And it is this effect that troubles me more than anything. The thought that I am her in some way, her ghost, her past. When she sees me, she sees all the reasons for her being as she is—that fierce bloated darkness that waddles and wobbles disarranged through the streets day and night.

She is who I am. Looking forward and looking back all in an instant whenever our paths cross. My eyes ask hers what I can possibly do to avoid becoming her, and her eyes beg me to do whatever I can to keep her from having to be. Those instances are worst of all. Those moments as we stare face to face, looking into and seeing nothing other than our mutual powerlessness, our unavoidable fate.

END OF THE CENTURY

social revolt has been numbed by
a conspiracy of circumstance

poverty so deep taking a good shit
is a luxury

gross national pootbutt: glorification of media whores
                                scabby bitches who don't use rubbers
                                who think douching's middle class
                                (coming generations will work
                                better to noise

if the spirit is chillin' and the crack don't rise)

i'm so busy writing the reviews
i can't begintoget to the nit-grit

ghetto mentality as extension of slave mentality
refried brains and thoughts the consistency of plantains

fear of type-casting as a
literary bureaucrat

worse, a rebop reject

when pussy loses its snap-back, its juice and friction rub
brings on a dick-bender

what does one do
when the race is over fo' you can
even get out the gate

AS AN ARBUS

bleeding from the shutter butt. weeds nourished
by tombstones/the latent life of a photograph
custom matte, a rich print (even tho the
negative is dirty and scratched)
this lost vision/icy sunshine thus

solitude is for the sheltered, the wealthy, the sane
(hairy mouths surround me, gab endlessly on theoretical
happiness, numb my ears)

if i crack the lens i may claim the voices
made me do it (the party line)
if i break my face who will care (the voiceless
can't be seen)

is this the dying in the effort? must be

rational approaches to life/unbleached poses
result only in poverty and confusion (stopped down)

study in black & white: one prime, overweight, neatly
dressed sepia woman. her kinky hair hidden in a
turban. she sits stiffly on an old divan which is
covered in plastic. her hands in flight, she frowns
mask-like at the fat tabby jumping spryly into her
skirted lap

ha-ha

■

frozen in the beam of headlights/eyes on hold
i lower my crossbow
he moves to me, licks my hand
his skin glistens streaming sweat
there's something else in this jungle
some other stranger danger
he starts and dashes back into the bush
i am left to face it alone

SECOND CLASS ANGEL

there's a part of heaven
reserved for my kind. the sun don't
grow there. the money don't shine

it's not about wings
altho chicken today feathers tomorrow
might be called a way of being

periodically
there's a breakthru: one of us
gets over polishing halos

evidentially
status has endless ramifications
like an infinite pecking order

which suggests

the light
one moves toward ascending in death
is merely the non-reflective neon of God's
corporate boardroom

OFFICE

for Fred Pollack

there the time clock's feverish ticks
there the bulging files full of static information
awaiting application
there the sturdy metal desk, upon it the word processor
with computer terminal and disc storage compartment
multiple metal filing trays, reference books
a pencil sharpener, pen & pencil holder, calendar
stapler, ashtray full of knick-knacks & paper clips
in-and-out trays, an anti-glare desk lamp
transcriber/dictator machine with special lite-wear
earphones, a box of snotkins, a half-eaten
chewy caramel nut bar, a cold cup of coffee grown over
with bacteria

a monster has eaten the secretary in this picture

intense focus on small things
keeps sane

UNFINISHED GHOST STORY (2)

this used to be her office.

it's chilly in here.

they've taken out some of the equipment and moved it
over to the new building.

what was she like?

quiet. a good worker, actually. but a loner—kind of
eccentric.

how so?

she was an odd dresser—head wraps, flashy jewelry—that
kind of thing. she wasn't very good at small talk. not a
gofer. it was her independent attitude, unsuited
to this kind of job.

what's that odor?

some cheap perfume. she always kept a bottle of it there in
the upper right hand drawer.

i've heard noises in here in the late afternoon. sometimes
the word processor clicks on by itself and begins typing.

yes. others have made the same complaint.

and Lopez, the security guard has seen her going in and
out of the ladies' restrooms. he's tried to catch her, but she
turns a corner and disappears.

yes. the boys in the mail room have bitched to
administration that she appears at 8 a.m. every Thursday
and deposits invisible mail into the slots.

what are they going to do about it?

corporate exorcism.

isn't that dangerous business?

routine, these days.

eagle gives birth to serpent
serpent consumes eagle
eagle eats thru and exits serpent
serpent expires and sustains eagle

DREAM 731

my hair in braids, i am dressed in a cloth of rainbow
i lay in a trance on a bed of pine which is covered
with a rainbow quilt. the bed is in a corner near
the fireplace in the one room of a log cabin. the cabin
sits atop the rainbow mesa. against the purple sky
i see rays of emerging sun. an eagle descends thru an
open window at the foot of the bed. i rise to receive
him. he plucks three sacred feathers from this his
incarnation. they too are of rainbow. he places them in
my cupped palms then flies away. i am taken by a nameless
joy. holding the feathers to my heart, i wake up
singing in an unfamiliar tongue

AUGURIES (4)

wind chimes patchouli wicker & sage

2 golden eagles locked in combat/coitus

a crimson rash

success diminished to outliving opposition

an ill-clad ancient rust-colored crone
babbling in tongue

hemeralopia

aurora borealis seen circling street lamps along
urban thoroughfares

the queen of swords

a black tenement burned to souvenirs after a shoot-out with
police. of eleven dead only one is a man

tachycardia

the failure of artificial suppressants
to take hold

the passing of water under stress followed by
sobs sans tears

living on java & dreams

smoke in the dark

i want to kill something

DREAM 924

the trip starts on the limitless freeway of my thoughts. the
tank is full. i am behind the wheel moving with undisturbed
swiftness. i feel the sigh of the engine, emanations through
the floor, my foot against the accelerator rises and falls as i
pass first on the left then on the right, swooping. lights
bobble in the fluid ink of night, amber, white and red street
stars. there is other life out there. i sense it, a smell, a
heat rising from my skin. i'm hugged in my black leather
jacket a perfect fit and fingerless black calfskin gloves. my
black kinks porcupine my scalp thickly, wild. my ears are
clamped in gold. my big hips hug the contoured seat and i
reach for the fake gearshift (because this vehicle really has
an automatic transmission) and i'm flying as the speedometer
needle presses urgently against the edge. ah — the power. i
am looking for the answer. and i move forward, my eyes
scoping the horizon as though a pinball course and i know
he's out here somewhere dead ahead enemy and lover. i am armed,
the beretta snug in the confines of my jacket. i think briefly
of the law. what if they give chase. but i've outrun them
        before.

i did not wake up today

NOSOMANIA

lawyer fever doctor flu

early symptom: inverted nipples/an unwillingness
                to respond

tongue of the jester—a lexicon of smiles and
entertainment styles/callus webbings of gossip and
misgivings—licks and slowly divests my mind
of protective soothe

        there's a gene for jealousy
        there's a gene for lying
        there's a gene for betrayal
        there's a genius for pain

so

lately my mad scramble has escalated to killer routine:

wake at cockcrow wash dress try to create comb hair drive
car get to the office slave slave steal an hour's break to
try and cut some slack slave slave go home walk in grabbing
food out the fridge to cook. cook. listen to the news listen
to his day return all calls serve dinner the kids need time
the mail begs the day's news listen to his day the phone
rings and rings and rings the thang breaks the what's it falls
over the dojigger collapses that craves that must i listen
to his complaint his day his need his time

ours

aftersex too spent to push it. i lay in the wet the
night the dark thinking i'll do it tomorrow there will be
enough time tomorrow fuck it tomorrow. stall for tomorrow
something good maybe

now

yawning hands to face listening to shower run hot
water listening to how i listen knowing there's a limit
to this a pound must be paid flesh his body and mine
his body against mine

burnt

periodic intermittent identity crises (mid brain anomaly)
this scrunch i'm trapped in/suffocates/an accumulation of
miseries doesn't allow stretch/cramps my smile/leaves no
bleeding space i'm walled in by skin a stifling cell
so tight

when i turn around i bump into myself

then

what must be found is the power to shake to cure
to return me to me

like ultimately

what is seen in the mirror
is all what is

as in
form dictates fate—

all the philosophy i need

A CIVILIZED PLAGUE

a friend and i were discussing the local scarcity
of decent apartments yet the abundance
of high-priced hell-holes. she complained the only
good ones at reasonable rates are units in which
the occupant has died of the virus

occasionally we hear what sounds like footsteps
on the ceiling. the joke is "it's the ghost"
until we remember the guy who lived here before us
he died of the virus
it is because of this, we suspect, we were able
to rent so quickly and easily
without a credit check

a friend & traveler says they're beginning to deny visas
to residents of
Los Angeles, New York and San Francisco

i was working/struggling to concentrate, depressed
about money madness when my matters were
interrupted by the crescendoing hallelujahs of
Handel's *Messiah* issuing vigorously from
my neighbor's stereo. it is
rumored he has the virus

NOTES OF A CULTURAL TERRORIST

angry. angry for days years decades. going to
explode so angry. born angry. why am i so
angry. talk about three piece suits and
polite silences

a staggering flood of images/impressions as
my tongue fails a bold and attention-getting statement

recollected statistics (4500 rejection slips)
racial incidents, socio-political conflicts, someone
maimed or dead

remember San Ysidro. remember Harvey Milk. remember
Eulia Love. remember MOVE

apparent senseless violence/the man and his wife
who went toe-to-toe blow-to-blow with The Law taking
school children hostage

not engendered to promo dialog and understanding
incidents i've personally experienced/penned the sordid
confessions of a shell-shocked bystander

seconds short and dollars shy

why/who do i keep threatening to kill? this
anger i carry within

rejection as intellectual as nigger as woman
as artist as fat as lotus lander as dirty
dick-licker as nigger as lover of black boys white boys
and jew boys as nonconformist as nigger nihilist
as a

person of such extremes. emotional violence
bitter. pending self-destruct

these are my fake pearls. i have no real ones

SPACE TRAVEL

for Vangelisti

over drinks at the airport (this, of course, is
another planet)

memories of the neo-uranian poet who
spent a good deal of time on venus but favored
the rigidity of self reflection. he died lusting
for that too fleet decade of polymorphism unleashed

"you don't know what a time that was for men"

a flight to somewhere

he was a poet flesh indulgent frequenting
jupitarian tea houses and saturnian moons
dug crank locker room and felching—the throes of
interplanetary fabulation

over alcohol and the risk of no arrival

the problem of sheathes rendered ineffective
by oil-based lubricants. the sock-shock of cold
showers. post modern celibacy the dreaded urgency of
self-love the resurgence of wedlock

"for men for men . . . you don't know"

rumors about the unprecedented rise in rapes
of nuns lesbians and elderly women
statistics inspired by fear

talk of sex over drinks at the airport bar. a new
heteroeroticism

memory of the bullet torn anus of Garcia Lorca
symbolism of relentless density. death on uranus
a too earthly contagium consuming
consumed him

on uranus. he said. there was. once life

GHOST OF MANIC SILENCE

yes, Camus said
death does

once a 20th century merlin, ah

but i swore i would cease to gibber/should not
till recognition was imminent — not for my
translucent beatic efforts but of my jet skin — both?

in dire truth i could not speak. one thousand saxophones
stilled. some evil word magician seized my eloquent
vibrato, would not let go/halted my seraphic loquaciousness
i was set upon by sinister malaise/pernicious dread ate
greedily of my brain, feasted on my melodic wind
got stumbling stinko in my ancient rain
dried up all emotive jizz. pyretic blisters crowded in
on my rogue tongue

my pristine word-faith sanguinely stained
my face became mask
my eyes dreary yellowed ellipses
my back curled and snaked

thus i remained a decade, more
when suddenly suddenly i was shaken from slumber
by the reveille of an angry race
i woke in an abomunist hissy

in time
to seize my final solitude

HAITIAN NIGHT

no names — please
desire's designated victim — all a conation
blood and semen

the boy in his seductive pose is
cancer is plague in lavender masque lost/a lie
an ending ending

the boy in the back of my eyes seduced by boys
in the back seat of that old pontiac/slain
before my eyes

epiphora. i will never be done crying

i will cry in the temple
i will cry in the street
i will cry in congress/scream my rage the splendid terror —
beat my breast

we're caught after dark, caught guard down
caught unawares
caught in the wrong box with the wrong answer

fast alley action or bath? private home or pleasure palace?
bar or bedroom?

pay pay pay for your play

> after it was over
> i was relieved and joyous. the
> distance between us did not matter
> surely for him it was the same

adrift near the dock: better suicide better suicide
suicide's better

confluent in the enveloping mist/melts into
the consuming murk/the muddy rim of eternity
leaves this womb for that other os/that bottomless throat
that sandpaper tongue
those all-seeing desperate orbs
float up

sans face

gouged out in blind horror

he is lost to the pus/blister/chancre — *kuru*
cursed

to that
cavern of skulls & bones in the cool rain of jungle dust and
    light

THE SECRET TONGUE OF THE GONE

squiggles divine the passage
the ancient formula of how to turn love into gold

i am lost in the twenty-story temple
unable to escape the mindfuck
and the muzak of solipsistic rebop (mundo lingo)

where is the astral bridge between this bang and the next?

talk to me talk to me talk me to death
end-organ

    see and i see nada
    see and i see

an ancient menstrual stain

play these unforgiving notes
blow them
on the ultimate horn of the big bad bard
resurrect that guru of groove who haunts the sleaze
leaves a trail of ectoplasm in the haunted halls of romance
to the beat of

one foot tap dancing

MESSAGE FROM XANADU

the henna-haired waif appears in a spinster's dream

disappears
as they pass the bemooned mirror

a disembodied wail/the merciless bleep of the monitor

that lady and her tabby familiar
begs coin along the avenue of stars

they don't speak about that skull-rattling
loneliness
they don't speak about
the light that devours thought
they don't speak
about that loathsome bone piercing cold

open de door let de debbil in
open de door let ol' debbil in
give 'em a quarter he'll give you a grin

dear darling die famous or don't die

AUGURIES (5)

nightshade tiger balm ash & talc

a puma sighted prowling city streets

yaws

a cornucopia of schemes to salvage sanity

a shot gun. pipe fittings.   a .45 slug
and a broom

palmar desquamation

the sudden unexplained leap of a sleepwalker
into rush-hour traffic

an inverted moon

on prime-time news an elderly caucasian male
suiciding in flood waters

siderosis

the irresistible urge to walk backwards
in rhythmic circles

clouds in fingernails

the extinction of a smile
with a joint

opiate induced orgasms

broken lines

rain and sun in the same skin

4

*in whose tongue the word forget
has no translation*

REGION OF DESERTS

1

i walk thru the eye of sun

the black boy moves toward me
we pass thru each other under palms dying
in hot dry august

an albino pigeon takes flight

everywhere shards of glass
angry fruitless shatterings of
bottles and barred store windows

                    protest

the rusted scarecrow of sign designating store hours
walls of blistered cracked peeling stucco
twisted rust red steel corpses of
abandoned autos

mexico reclaims this desolation

2

where my shattered heart pines

home   to liquor stores & churches on every corner
            to dark red & gold wall-papered holes
            of refuge
            to stark welcoming envelopes of
            food stamps & government stipends
            to mom & pop stores with their counters of
            stinking stale meat & overripe fruit
            to black & white armored knights
            slaying for want of dragons

home   to boarded up remnants of memory
              to find them broken into/violated

3

that grinning wino mama time, snaggletoothed
rocks the sacred rock
stirred by rooster grape crowing
in her vessels
preaches from her bible of
cock-crow woes

i am a visitor here

a haint

              (i didn't know i'd gone till i came back didn't
              know i couldn't come back till i'd gone. now
              i know i can no longer bear the heat)

i am the 14-year-old fat black girl
entering the AAA theatre which was totaled 18 years ago

i order hot buttered popcorn and a suicide

home   to the continual R&B of curbed low riders
              the cabled redwood crucifixes of pacific telephone
              pale canary fire hydrants cracked open gushing
              forth the city's pale blue fluoridated blood

i am a haint here

5

                              "all dat booty! i bet
                              yo ol' man have a gud
                              ti-i-i-me"

292

i was in such a
big hurry i didn't
notice flowers bloom
or trees twist skyward
or the muffled pain of my children
in such a big fuckin' rush
i couldn't see anything
but that ape shit gorilla on my back
roarin' and snortin'
in so big a hurry to kick king kong
i was in the middle of the street
'fore i noticed the light was red

6

goin' somewheres?

the closer you get to the oasis
the lighter skins become

7

take good care of that
smile, now
when i see her again
i want to see
her smile

whatever happened to waco?
22 used to bar tend in them far out
afro numbers down at the brass rail and
shoot pool with the guys
when business was slow. she
nevah could draw a draft without puttin'
a head on it so big
the whole damned mug was foam

whatevah happened to waco
with her high behind ten feet off earth
them too fine licorice thighs
and honeysuckle tits?
remembah the fit she threw time
ace joker had her and kathy workin'
his table 'n tipped kathy a dollar
and gave waco one red cent!

whatevah happened to waco?
and those big brown eyes/starved dogs
bayin' moonrise to moonrise

8

goin' somewheres?

only junkies wear overcoats
in 90 degree weather

haint

9

at the bone the meat is dry and old
34 swims in red sauce
there's only two customers in the ghetto
rib joint
the 3 fates runnin' it must be losin' money
lessin' they got a side hustle
the sauce is
hot & sweet at the same time
(like me, my love say)

10

      goin' somewheres?

miz big hurry
in such a rush
dead before she know it

11

home.   (i am a visitor)

the firecracker fart of exhaust
traffickin' down manchester avenue
it looks worse every time i come here it looks worse
all but closed down
all the biz-zi-ness goin' out of business
all the new shine gone
nothin' left but rust, dust
and the cracked bones of a dream

in the eye of sun
i burst into particles of pain
scatter everywhere across the
disappearing present

look close

the memory of my shadow can be found
clinging to bleached slum walls

i am a haint here

settled in the sand of its past
my skull grins

BAKERSFIELD USA

i zero in on *el dorado* push that fire engine red mustang
to the floor. we take that high mountain pass at mach one
Chuck Man at my side is *loosiana* drunk nodding out and
i'm in a hurry to see what's shaking on the love horizon

all we got's twenty dollars in change and no change of clothes
the adventure of good air and green valley something in our
genes rips the heart out of ripe california melons and giggles
like juveniles as we run through that landscape of cotton and i
pick it for the first time

and Chuck's eyes pleasure up and down my paper-thin black
sateen backless mini my long long maple legs and can't wait to
get me off into the first juke we can spot in our part of town

if you ever go to a strange place, sugar, all you have to do
is find and follow one of us and you'll be safe

we turn heads at the mighty white do-right cracker eatery on
sunday morning for slow service funking up the gray boy
interior with our motel monkey fuck musk and it's all
outrageous fun as Chuck goes into his geechie act

underneath i feel his stomach churn hankering for another half
pint and begging me please please don't be so harsh in my
judgment

you can survive an earthquake if you know how

THE WAIF OF ECHO PARK

I'm surprised by Monica's call. We don't know each other very well. We were mutual friends of a lady gone on. She insists on talking and I take the time.

She says she heard Susannah's ghost knocking about after a prayer. She scolded Monica for the summons then busted her toilet, the one her old boyfriend fixed, the guy Susannah didn't like.

She burns candles for her.

She occasionally cries until she chokes on regret. She berates herself because she didn't fully understand Susannah's predicament. *None of us could save her,* I think, *she coulda saved herself but she opted out.*

I describe those last moments in the hospital again, reliving Susannah's awkwardness and surprise, her embarrassment about her appearance, the cumbersome tubes, her dismay at being unable to speak. How, when she tried to write she made nonsensical swirls beyond all language.

She listens but anxiously interrupts with more to tell. About this talk radio psychic. Monica called him up that morning. She wanted a reading done on her dog. Which is why she's calling me in the first place. The psychic zoned in on her dog. Her dog complained she was unhappy and smoked too much. Her dog didn't approve of so much smoking. Then she asked if the psychic did humans. He said he did sometimes and so she asked about Susannah. He threw her in for free.

He said she'd had a severely painful death. It was a suicide. A health-related suicide. "She was ashamed of something she did." And then he said "it" was responsible. And then he asked her, "Who's 'H'?" She didn't know.

I know. I get a chill. I'd heard Susannah had been chippin' again.

And then he said Susannah pointed at her vagina, that it's highly unusual for the departed to point to the genitalia. "It means she was deeply hurt by her husband, a hurt she never recovered from."

297

She doesn't know what that means. I get another chill. I know about this also although, again, I offer no explanation.

And then he said, "She wants you to take care of 'B,' whatever that means." We both know exactly who that means. And she cried into the receiver because she could not afford to fulfill Susannah's wish. I consoled her.

"But one more thing," she told me, "he said she's happy where she is. The psychic didn't say where. Just that she's happy."

After we hung up I sat and wondered. Perhaps she is happy. At last. It's a corny sentiment which hurts no one.

SAN DIEGO

"the light is like this
in the south of France," he says

we stand on the pier
watch the blond boys afloat
with their surfboards
waiting to ride the big wave

"here i can be somebody," he says

a wave comes and two of the boys take it in

the boys. how well tanned they are
with skins the color of wet sand
poised unconcerned
in aryan uniformity

"you breathe better here. the air
is pure. we can rent a house off the beach"

we listen to the roar
another wave. more boys take it in
my heart *hangs ten,* braces with the wet thrill
of foam as they splash graceful
into the shallows

"you can find work here easily. me too," he says

i answer absently, my eyes on the blond boys

"this is a military town, full of rednecks
a tougher lily white town than the one i come from
and i don't swim"

satin slate pelicans perch atop the lamps
that dot the pier. charcoal and enamel gulls dive
back and forth ocean-side

and cream white crests of waves crash
along the most unspoiled beach i've ever seen

his eyes my eyes. his lips mine
afterwards the light is brighter. we look out
into the rainbow of blues greens and aquamarines
watch as laughing swimmers return

"i guess you have a point," he says

we make our way silently along
glistening rocks. the waves roar

i pick sand stones
to carry home

ON THE OTHER END OF MELROSE

bruja y palma

always it is dusk
vampira haunts the antimatter
there's no parking at the rose cafe
lovers tongue beneath a traffic-clogged freeway underpass
a gourmand's choice of thai-chinese, chilean empanadas or
      spinach crepes
the dope dealer does his do from a black-on-white corvette
film crews shoot break-dance sequences (he will leave you
      he has always left you)
as black-laced mantillas scurry home from storefront
      worship of the virgin holy mama
the headless corpse of fresh killed cock twitches
      in averted eyes
a block-long limo lands in front of mars and rock stars exit
      for the mix
halfway house escapees snore on bus stop benches
as Priapus takes a solo promenade
all questions go unanswered
always it is dusk

INVITATION TO A GUNFIGHTER

you rode into town on a mighty tall horse, Durango
and now it's time for that last showdown

and the townspeople who sired you
have all turned against you
in their arrogance ignorance and fear
and the subject of your love
is as fickle as the wind

and you're punch-drunk as a skunk in a trunk
looting and shooting for pleasure — tearing up
their peace of mind

and they're all too scared to take you on —
the gutless lot of 'em

and you're too bitter and fed up with the bad hand
fate has dealt you in the form of black skin
and deadly aim

it's time to get out of town, Durango
time to get the first thang smokin'
go on and get on
to whatevah is waitin' in that wild wild way out yonder

time to take that long slow technicolor ride

before they ambush you in the saddle
and leave you face up in the sun

302

AUGURIES (6)

adder's-tongue jacaranda rosewood & oak

a dog awalk on three legs

black emesis

a glut of verbiage emotional cul-de-sacs & truculent eyes

the disembodied yeeaahhh
of an alien baritone

vitiligo

the abrupt appearance of formless insects
amove in a spiral at the foot of a bed

one-eyed jills

a millionaire slumlord found hanging
from the knotted end of his aryan dream

catalepsy

the traumatic stress release of
feculent wind

a jitter jag

whispered warnings from walls

the grinning christ
in a bodega window

blood of the shaman — head of the crow

SELF-IMMOLATION

it takes a peculiar kind of anger
centuries of racial stress
concentrated into a bitter lifetime's struggle
frustration/failure to accomplish
it takes a certain tone of skin
thinned under repeated ironings by a dense oppression
it takes the anguish-soaked wick of the heart
the fuel of soul sickened beyond
self-love
and some trigger—the flint of a wrong word said
the match of a sudden sharp loss
or the tortuous death of an ideal

then come smoke
then come flame

EASTER SUNRISE

in black down the deserted avenue of god i trod
song of my feet/litany for the mad
bereaved

the bells ring
los angeles opens palm thighs
receives the sun

> let us all go
> to the grave
> in fucking's ecstasy

my lover sleeps on the roadside
his way back to me the long winding drive toward sanity
wags and twists a mother's tongue/dialogue
between doper and dopee: birth of the worm

> let us all go fuck
> ecstasy is the grave

> clang clang clang

in black
i trod the avenue thumbs up
it'll cost you
more than a song
more than bells ringing

> deaf to the beauty of his dream

question re stupidity: why are the mundane so quick to reject
the different

> *i might catch it*

flesh fall
first a finger like a small elongated stone

then the nose
lost, one precious proboscis coveting odor
an eye
freed of encasement within the skull
freed at last
to float in the chemist's beaker

(looking for the cause)

> clang clang clang
> damned bells damned church
> damned cult of flesh damned needle
> damned skin

signature of acceptance: tongue to vagina

mother forgive them
they know exactly what they do

> (greater love hath no man than love for his woman)

blasphemy the needle blasphemy the needle blasphemy the
needle's blasphemy

mutter hail moneys
ave corporate entities

credit him
credit him
credit him

stuffed yellow baby chicks
a giant pink rabbit with two huge white front teeth
they found the child strangled
tested for sexual molestation

how to get away with robbery: tell'em two black guys did it
how to get away with murder: tell'em two black guys did it

> (they went thataway)

one black mind + one white appearance = CONFUSION

the bells tell me the cramps come in waves now more
        infrequent
as the days recede they peal out my love/hunger to go
        back to
him. at midnight those damned bells begin/summon the sun

today it arrived prematurely

against nature/the bells
bring down the sky
it lays about me
broken pieces/his laugh
i wade thru him
am bitten by fear

                ashes be ashes
                dust be dust

ave corporate entity
hail money

                house of the lord special
                tuesday wash
                hot wax baptism, $2.50
                with full tank

glory be to the father/law
        the son/mercy
        and the holy gun

        (chapter and verse i love you)

salvation is the name of the game

he was well hung
        by the noose
of white christian america
        until long after death

and his body
                burned in an open field
to forestall
                reawakening

                    clang clang clang

easter AM

the white rabbit on the roadside
thumbs north
that demon driver waves cold bones of a hand
gives him a lift
along the avenue of deserted gods
i pause, light the candle
in veiled distance
bells the clang of bells and
crazed laughter

THE ARTICLE IN THE NEWSPAPER

he says it's important news about the virus
and reads it to me

it's a habit we've acquired over our years
together and while i prefer to read
some things myself i don't mind his gesture
of affection

it reminds me of the day mother quit reading
to me and told me i was big enough to do it
myself. it reminds me of papa reading from the
bible before breakfast on sunday mornings. it
reminds me of how i used to sneak and go thru the
dresser where mama hid the dirty paperbacks; how i'd
speed read them and sneak them back unnoticed

today's article is one more of many we've read
discussing the virus. it claims it's man-made and
induced. we read in horror
it has the usual impact these articles do. we
feel glad we found each other (in time). and then we
think about the lovers we had
just before we hooked up

and wish them good health

NOSOMANIA (2)

the news reports about health professionals
accidentally contracting the virus
bring her to mind

i was eleven. the student nurse on
county hospital children's ward was a molasses-skinned
sistuh long on attitude. she hated to touch
and never shook hands. i watched the time
she embarrassed one father by refusing his
show of thanks. her smile was warm she
spoke kindly softly but contrariwise kept her stingy arms
folded, hands tucked at her waist.
confused, he nevertheless accepted her peculiar
behavior. when he left the room i jammed her

pulvinus eyes on fire she thralled me

about *disease*

how sick the world how nasty people how filthy
infested with all kinds of transmittable damnations
some of godly cause without cure

scared simple i kept my hands rigidly to myself
for months after discharge, even afraid to kiss mother
till worry wore me out

i finally dismissed her
wondering how one lived without touching

THE HOUSE OF BLUE LIGHTS

1

i find it at 5 AM in the cincinnati rain
the raw promise of dreamless sleep
(he is two thousand miles away)
there is a vision in these dark windows/flesh
doing the slow grind the funky butt the low down
dirty dog. i am hungry for the beat
can sniff it. it is black slick wet and dark eyes
me in the bottle of my solitude/a half pint
such a cheap high. otis redding moans
            "try a little tenderness"

they are searching for the man
with a missing sinister finger

i am homesick. stricken suddenly
i head for the streets/afton/niggah town
where my fine brown belongs
i speak in tongue and pray in blues

it is here. for you. the moist cool os of pearl
it is here for you. my youth and my dying. it is here. for
        you
a millennium of please. it is here for you. this opium/stuff
wisdom. for you

it is said the blind man sips monkey through a straw
and they are dragging the mississippi
for victims of the man
with the finger missing from his sinister hand

don't let me die too soon

there is no sun here. there is no moon
the tables are small and behold blood red candles
his hunger comes in on the bassoon solo. sure he wants

a young tender, not a tough old hen like me
but he has chosen
and i render

there is a shattering of mirrors
the dark substance love runs down my arm

everywhere they seek the man with the finger missing
from his sinister hand

and i am drowning in morning haze
in the house of blue lights
in the cold sweat of need

2

crazy for the wild love of night

the joint is done in wine and gold
chandeliers tinkle/ice cubes in a water-back
it goes down warm satin swan
and the rage abates. the purr is on
the mist rolls in. i am ready for flight
be the duke of juke
lead me there. run a dollar in quarters
dance me till i drop

3

take 7 hairs from the head of a bitter woman
soak in alcohol for 7 days
stitch them into his pillow
if he stays beyond the 7th night
he is yours forever

burn a black candle in the morning
burn a red candle at noon
sweep round the bed twice

sprinkle it down with fine ground root
johnny conqueror
none can draw him from you

drink 7 glasses of woe
turn on the radio
sleep until his blood wakes you

MOTHER THE FLESH

has no logic
knows no reason
its tongue his tongue my tongue
tongues. nations

> *he is peach*
> *i am hot cocoa red*

ocean our sweat swells threatens this small island/bed
danger of drowning so real

mother flesh

knows no season. springs forth age after ice age
defies time form climate. is isomorphic
cycles of being felt in cellular rhythm & blues so essential

> blood vs stone

spins shakes trembles tremors rots rejoices burns boils fails
feels corrupts conquers hurts hungers maddens moves
withers wonders pains pleases asks answers
dares damns dreams

dear mama the flesh

i know. knowing does not control. you know. how long with
papa? with poverty? raising us almost alone
nights crying while we clung to the tv those creditors
taking your blood for his. the other partners. late hours
the sweatshop cold settling into your shoulders
vacant aspirations. then know me

> *he is sea fresh sand*
> *i am fine shellacked cedar*

mother flesh

314

births neon neolithic necropolises where the young feed well
the old flee the night. a piss pool of struggle
my eyes disembodied orbs scope the horizon/spirit blight
the metalloid lovers who bang on the boulevards
grasp at it glory in it

blood on stone

mama the meat

is why. is sustenance. strengthens. makes best nada
hip to hip. sperm & egg. muscle music. sweet sweet sweet
tastes like roses smell. goes down gentle. satisfies head
heart hope and the god eye. sanctifies

(suckafo'lovesuckafo'lovesuckafo'love)

he is apricot silk
i am cinnamon tea

ma flesh is

the battleground on which truth is ever victor

bloodstone

now i enter the temple. such walls. they tower
humbled i feel yet a speck yet a consciousness/
consuming ALL

kneel

he is with me
yet away from me
in me
yet outside of me
one

it's good. it's good. it's good

mother
the flesh forgives everything

BLACK ISIS

for Michael Palmer

undergoing ecstasy a woman sings and plays jazz piano
knowing thousands will be healed as she performs

she has two thoughts about this
if she should stop they would succumb to entropy

if she continues her virtuosity will enlighten them
in the second case the first thought is erased

causing great joy

in this instance of song

she would know her darkest self
her belly grown fat with the urgency of life

> *my being is exalted*
> *glistens with the sweat of my labor's magic*

such thoughts recreate the world
and this is good

PAEAN TO DARK BARS

Dark bars are female, sumptuous holes, sometimes stark, dense atmospheres with smells thick as menstrual blood. Get lost here get found. Be in comfort be welcomed, "unlax" from the world. It's keep-up-with, own the jones, dope to the bones. Let go among others albino to jet. The stink of sweat soaked walls, the textures of furniture stained with grease from kitchens exuding the magic of deep fat fryers and grilled delights. An air tinged with the stale remnants of a multitude of smokes and the pungent vapors of heady libations.

Partake of ritual. Meet and be met.

Watch a dark man enter a dark bar. Watch how he surveys the turf. How he finds his spot and marks it. How he radiates troubles or the need to be alone. Read his weariness or his eagerness to be involved, social. Check out his walk. Direct and self assured, loosely disjointed, or cautiously erect. Check out the cut and fit of his clothes, how he breathes. What he does with his hands—jangles his car keys in his pocket, goes immediately into his inner pocket for cigarettes, nails clean, polished or grimy with the signature of his workplace. How his face finds the appropriate configuration transmitting need. Or disappointment. Does he sigh or is he silent, allowing his eyes to speak for him, does he immediately mouthily establish his presence.

Watch a dark woman enter with a dark man. Does he ring her waist with his arm. Are they arm-in-arm. Does he escort her in first, holding back the door. Does she wait while he picks their "spot" or does she lead while he follows, satisfied with her choice. Do they sit for an instant, undecided, then get up and move from booth to counter or counter to booth. And do they go immediately into conversation. Or does he take her hand. Do they nuzzle. Or do they lean back against the soft leather of their seats. Is she attentively quiet when he speaks or boisterous. How long before she gets up to go to the ladies' room. Does she go to the juke box and when. After drinks are served or before. And as she approaches the box does she pause

317

just a moment, her ass toward his face, making a bald suggestion. Does he watch her walk, take in her shape, and lean back or forward. Does he smile, in memory or anticipation. Or does he look down into his glass leaving her to the casual eyes of others.

Watch a dark woman enter alone. Does she go immediately to the ladies' room, stay for a time, then languidly make her repeat entrance. Is her walk cat-like or her heels ratta-tat-tat. Does she head immediately for a stool to order a drink. Does she assume a booth alone. Does she take out her purse, find and fire a cigarette. Does she order a beer or a cocktail. If a beer, does she use a glass or drink it from the bottle. When she gets her drink does she down it impatiently or nurse it slowly. At the juke does she linger, make her selections casually, does the music entice her to movement. Should a man offer quarters does she play them and does he request a dance. Does she accept.

Do they move on to the dance floor alone or are they amid other couples. Do they find their way into the center or linger at the edge. Is it a slow number or fast, blues or rhythm. Does he watch the gyrations of her body closely. Does he match hers with his. Does he measure her curves against his muscular angles. Does she look beyond his eyes, the broadness of his shoulders, the taper at his waist, below. If the number is slow, does he pull her in to him or keep her at a respectable distance. Does he signal his moves with his left hand at the small of her back. Does he whirl her romantically, does he lock her to him, gripping her arm short of pain, and grind against her for all he's worth. Does he sweat, does she, does their sweat mingle. When the number is over, does she rush away from him, avoiding his eyes. Does she allow him to escort her to her table. Does he thank her, gentlemanly, and walk away.

As she returns to her table do eyes follow eagerly. As her songs play does she smoke looking off into space, or do her eyes seek prospects. And when a man approaches, perhaps another man, does she invite him to join her. Does she ignore him until he goes.

Last call for alcohol.

Does the dark night seem darker spent alone. Does the hunger loosen inhibitions. Is it true even ugly is transformed when lights dim and the minute hand approaches closing. Does

318

the air bristle with lust aroused yet unsated. As the last number is played, do couples rush to the floor embracing as much against the dark as in it. Will the cold that comes with sunup bring satisfaction or regret.

but, ruby my dear

he hikes those narrow chords one more time
to a dingy walkup on the outskirts of ecstasy
he knows every note of her
down to that maddening musky treble
from between her dusky thighs
even as he raps twice to let her know
he means business
and hears her singeful "who's there?"
as she unlocks the double bass count
he's gonna put hurt on her
he's gonna love her like winter loves snow
he's gonna make her
beyond that scratchy 78 whining dreary days and
whiskey nights
beyond that too sweet smoky andante
beyond that hunger for impossible freedom
to the heart of melody
where they will go to steam
in the jazzified mystical sanctity
of discordant fusion

scaling

"when you eat the chosen one
he will transform you"—Circe

SCYLLA & CHARYBDIS

this sargasso muddied with the blood
of a thousand variegated lovers
whirls and sucks

some whooowhee

a current obsessed draws him in
the promise of no escape (a tree long felled)

this woman deep water this woman siren
this man this war this man's voyage

so unlike Odysseus

she covers his head his eyes whited back
in crisis tongue slack, wordless
stiffened arms his body swirling
in the rigors his joining joy birth
drowning

flesh and the rendering of it flesh
and his surrender to it (sailor sailor
home. at last. for a pearl) laughter born of
release having encountered the monster, embraced
her been consumed by her come in her
wet sated whole and washed ashore

his names for my breasts

SWEET MAMA WANDA TELLS FORTUNES
FOR A PRICE (3)

my man's arms
hold me/we fill the city
his strength
fires me
here we're to love

he stays
he helps
he conjures

day breaks into
tears/shakes
into my shoulder
night our lips
sigh, tongues dance

at last
into each other
we are. and
know
to the stone bone

this tomorrow

AFRICAN SLEEPING SICKNESS (2)

orgasmic psychosis — coming and nevah coming
down

a temporary temporal paralysis terrifying in sudden onset
holds me soundless fighting to break its hold

say they say they

(something long dug into my brain making
hammer blows beneath my cranium)

spots appear before my eyes. i go into a faint
twist slowly to the floor losing consciousness for
brief seconds. startled observers rush to my aid
something in my mouth
keeps me from swallowing my tongue

fear is on me paregoric in passion
i am seized by a spell of dry heaves. later my stomach
seeks exit thru my lower intestines

say this confusion say love

or one could simply say the anatomy of lust is soft
wet and pink (each lover making off with his favorite
part)

at-home-in-bed fever
the skin on my lips tightens begins to peel and flake
my eyes itch threatening to swell palms red
unaccountable throbbings below

sing to me

between my thighs runs the river whiskey and he — he is a
divin' duck

what i know of my man

how his head turns when desire enters his mind
how he smells me how my smell arouses how he absorbs my
breasts legs buttocks how my feet, hands and nails
evoke touching how the color and textures of my skin
agitate how in black lace i stir his saint, white
his beast, red the john, blue the romantic
how his eyes experience and transmit entry imagined
how his ears taste my hot breath and listen acutely
for expressed fantasies how his nose opens how
his too moist mouth broods over my nipples
how his dickhead tears in worship how he sometimes
pauses to savor my anticipation how his
adventuresome tongue explores and excites my rapture
how his blood rushes how our bodies glow together how
friction exacerbates his final exquisite suffusion

baby baby

GIVE ME TIME

for Austin

give me jazz afternoon
give me slow sun in a glass eye
& a long drag on a j of bo
give me deep breath deep breath deep breath
a sip of california may wine
give me a reflective mocking smile
& breath. a deep breath
another catch of sweet sun
another toke on the j
more wine
california may wine
turn up the jazz
another breath. dancing
a breath dancing in the wine
high. tension gone
the sun smiling in the jazz
this afternoon
thinking of you. and laughing
as breath comes sweet as wine
california may wine
and thoughts of loving you
take me so high
even jazz can't go there

AMERICAN SONNET (2)

for Robert Mezey

for outshining the halos of heaven's greedy archangels
the sensitive nightfall with her dazzling teeth
is sentenced to the eclipse of eternal corporate limbo
the exquisite isolation of endless neon-lit hallways

for the miscegenation of her spirit to earth's blood
for giving her moonrises to tropical desires
powerful executives syphon off her magic
to face the consequences of devilish exploitation

towards the cruel attentions of violent opiates
as towards the fatal fickleness of artistic rain
towards the locusts of social impotence itself

i see myself thrown heart first into this ruin

not for any crime
but being

THE SWEETENING

blighted bones sharpen, pierce gratified flesh
black blackens still

eyes deepen with irrevocable woe
sickness
redemption's soft rot — failed organs
a sluggish current of accumulations
oceans oceans tighten skin
(stock footage of leaves rustling in
october wind)

a door long shut opens
the bed occupied by uncanny brightness
(the rendering of greed of want)
a true dissolution of concern
puts the world away quietly
gently

neatly folded
smelling of sunshine

hear the singing

■

when i sense the shadow
i step on his hand to keep him still
and promise in a whisper
to always remember
turning away, i release him
and do not follow

at midnight i go to the closet

Printed October 1990 in Santa Barbara & Ann
Arbor for the Black Sparrow Press by Graham
Mackintosh & Edwards Brothers Inc. Text set in
Baskerville by Words Worth. Design by Barbara Martin.
This edition is published in paper wrappers;
there are 300 hardcover trade copies;
125 hardcover copies have been numbered & signed
by the author; & 26 handbound in boards by Earle
Gray are lettered & signed by the author.

Photo: Susan Carpendale

A native of Los Angeles, Wanda Coleman presently works as a medical secretary. She has received literary fellowships from the National Endowment for the Arts and the Guggenheim Foundation in the past; most recently, a literary fellowship from the California Arts Council. She is best known for her dramatic performances, having given hundreds of readings in the United States and overseas. A recording artist as well, her first solo release is *High Priestess of Word* (New Alliance/BarKubCo). She co-hosts "The Poetry Connexion," an interview program with Austin Straus for Southern California's Pacifica radio station. She is winner of the 1990 Harriette Simpson Arnow Prize for fiction, presented by *The American Voice*. She continues to publish from her growing body of fiction and some essays as well. *African Sleeping Sickness* is her sixth book; the author has revised *Mad Dog Black Lady* for this edition.